A School for Every Child
School Choice in America Today

Edited by Sandra Harris
and Sandra Lynn Tillman Lowery

scarecrow
education

A Scarecrow Education Book
The Scarecrow Press
Lanham, Maryland, and London
2002

A SCARECROW EDUCATION BOOK

Published in the United States of America
by Scarecrow Press, Inc.
A Member of the Rowman & Littlefield Publishing Group
4720 Boston Way, Lanham, Maryland 20706
www.scarecroweducation.com

4 Pleydell Gardens, Folkestone
Kent CT20 2DN, England

British Library Cataloguing in Publication Information Available

Library of Congress Cataloging-in-Publication Data
A school for every child : school choice in America today / edited by Sandra
    Harris and Sandra Lynn Tillman Lowery.
        p. cm. — (A Scarecrow education book)
    Includes bibliographical references.
    ISBN 0-8108-4188-6 (pbk : alk. paper)
    1. School choice-United States. I. Harris, Sandra, 1946– II. Lowery,
        Sandra Lynn Tillman, 1944–
    LB1027.9 .S357 2002
    379.1'11'0973-dc21   2001041921

♾™ The paper used in this publication meets the minimum requirements of
American National Standard for Information Sciences-Permanence of
Paper for Printed Library Materials, ANSI/NISO Z39.48-1992.
Manufactured in the United States of America.

*The editors want to acknowledge and especially thank
Dr. Garth Petrie for his daily support and encouraging mentorship
throughout this book project and in our professional lives.*

Contents

Section One
Overview
1

Chapter One
Legal Aspects of School Choice Issues
9

Section Two
Public Schools of Choice
19

Chapter Two
Magnet Schools
21

Chapter Three
Charter Schools
33

Chapter Four
Public Alternative Schools
45

Chapter Five
Public Schools and Private Profit:
The Challenge of Educational Management Organizations
53

Section Three
Private Schools of Choice
73

Chapter Six
The Independent School
75

Chapter Seven
Catholic Schools
87

Chapter Eight
Christian Schools
99

Chapter Nine
Homeschools
109

Section Four
Choosing Wisely for Our Children
127

Chapter Ten
What to Look for in Good Schools
129

Conclusion
145

Contributors
149

Overview

Sandra Harris, Ph.D.

- Che was in his second attempt at ninth grade and still not doing well. Last night, he had stayed after school hoping someone would help with his math, but no one was available. He wanted to do well, but he just couldn't. He was tall and wanted to play on the basketball team, but why try out? Che was rarely successful at school.

- Sonia was the only girl in her sixth-grade class who hadn't been invited to the birthday party. Why didn't the other girls like her? Was it because she was the only black girl in the class? Or was it because she made straight As? Sonia awakened every morning feeling sad that she had to go to school.

- Tom was a sophomore. He had participated in the Duke University Talent Search in middle school and had scored very well. His predicted SAT score was in the 1400s, but his grades were just average. He could play nearly every musical instrument and would wake up at night with the music of a new song in his head. He just couldn't get excited about school the way he got excited about music.

- Until this year when John entered middle school he had loved school. He was a really good student, not very athletic, and a bit overweight. Now, every day when he came in from school he complained to his mother that "some guys" were going to beat him up. John was afraid to go to school.

- Kim began speaking in clear sentences by the time she was 14 months old. What a smart baby! She had energy to burn; in fact, by the time she entered kindergarten, her pediatrician had prescribed Ritalin to slow her down a bit. As a fourth grader, she finished her work long before the other students, and when she did there was nothing to do. So she talked, or tried to help another student, or walked around the room. Sometimes, something out in the hall would catch her attention and she would go investigate. Kim didn't like to go to school because it seemed that she was in trouble most of the time.

Che, Sonia, Tom, John, and Kim are real kids who have not found success in traditional public schools. As recently as 10 years ago, unless their parents could move into a new school attendance zone, the primary option available to them was a tuition-based private school. But, today:

- Che is enrolled in a parochial school where he is a member of the basketball team and getting tutored in math.

- Sonia is enrolled in an inner-city public charter school and, while still making straight As, she is surrounded with friends.

- Tom will graduate this year from a public magnet school that emphasizes music and the arts.

- John is in a Christian school where he is not afraid; in fact, he's the president of the student council.

- Kim is attending a public charter school especially designed for kids with special learning needs. She still gets in trouble some of the time, but feels much better about herself because, at her new school, "Kids here are like me."

Reform Movement in Education Today

In the 1960s and 1970s, parental dissatisfaction with local school campuses resulted in some school districts creating alternative and magnet schools. These schools allowed children to enroll from a variety of attendance zones and frequently offered special programs serving specialized groups, such as gifted or at-risk students (Choice and Vouchers, 2000). Education in the 21st century is still experimenting with different school structures. Nationally, the movement for basic change in education continues to direct school reform efforts.

Much of this has come about as a result of school reform literature, which has encouraged the reexamination of forms of schooling. Today's trend for educating children is often a hands-on, value-driven, close-to-the-customer small school with a personal client-centered focus, resulting in more educational options. Increasingly, the picture of education in America today is no longer a "head to head" public school versus private school issue. Instead, it is becoming a "hand in hand" partnership, as public and private entities work together to create different educational opportunities for our children under the umbrella of "school choice."

In response to the need to restructure schools, school choice has become a major topic in education today. For many years the concept of school choice only included the choice between the traditional neighborhood public school and private schools. Today the concept of school choice is wide ranging and includes a variety of options for parents as well as for educators. In addition to private schools of choice, which include independent private schools, parochial schools, and other schools that are supported by churches or synagogues, there is a growing trend for public schools to provide choice schools. Public schools of choice share two common components: They are supported by taxpayer expense, and they have some level of independence from local governing school boards. Choice opportunities within public school districts allow parents to decide which school within the district they would like to send their children, such as schools-within-schools, alternative schools, career academies, magnet schools, or charter schools. Generally, charter schools are run independently of the district, yet these nearly 1,700 publicly financed schools must have district or state approval to exist.

Illustrative of the growth of these public schools of choice, just since 1992, 37 states, including the District of Columbia, now offer parents and teachers a choice. In Cleveland, Milwaukee, and Florida, eligible students can select private schools, including religious schools, through voucher programs that are taxpayer-financed. In Arizona, Iowa, Illinois, and Minnesota, families can use tax credits to help cover costs incurred in a private education (Olson, 2000). The growth of homeschooling has increased by over 30% just within the last 10 years (Hawkins, 1996). More and more public school districts are creating special interest magnet schools with curricula that focus on business, health careers, the performing arts, and many more subjects. The options provided by school choice for parents to consider for their children are growing. School choice options are also giving educators more input in where to focus their professional lives.

Our world today is increasingly diverse and complex, and our nation's children reflect this diversity and complexity in their abilities and in their needs. In an effort to prepare children to be successful in the 21st century, school choice in America is offering parents opportunities to look beyond the attendance zone school and find the best fit for their child. Because of this, there are many factors today that influence parents' choice of schools. Certainly, parents and teachers want academic excellence for all children. But, additionally, parents consider other factors, including, safety, proximity, and teacher qualifications (Public Agenda, 1999). Other parents indicate that values taught and size of the school are influencing factors in deciding where they want their children to go to school. Schools today are moving beyond the "one size fits all" mentality and are creating a wide variety of schooling opportunities because education in a democratic society is less an issue of "what is best for schools" and more an issue of "what is best for kids."

These increased options in schooling have also broadened opportunities for teachers and administrators. Educators are also considering educational matters, such as curricula, teaching, class size (Finn, Manno, & Bierlein, 1996), and job satisfaction, and autonomy, influence, and freedom in the classroom (Bomotti, Ginsberg, & Cobb, 1999; Harris, 2001) in deciding where they will work. Choice is occurring at a time when competition for teachers and administrators from school to school is great.

How Do Parents and Educators Choose?

There is much confusion surrounding school choice issues. Because the majority of individuals sending their children to school today are products of the public school system, frequently parents and educators feel almost disloyal if they even consider looking at a school other than their neighborhood school. Other parents and individuals support the traditional neighborhood school because it is often the main identifier of the local community and there is a concern about losing "good kids" to other communities. Sometimes these feelings of support for the local school are founded on a basic concern for change, itself, often voiced as, "It was good enough for me, it should be good enough for my child." Polls indicate that while Americans think private schools offer a better education, most parents, as well as educators, still think local public schools do a good job and want to support them (Public Agenda, 1999). In this same poll nearly four out of five parents strongly agreed that they should have the right to choose the school they want their child to attend. One father commented, "There are some generic disadvantages to public school. It's one size fits all, and the parents have little choice" (Public Agenda, 1999, p. 24).

However, most Americans are clearly do not have a clear understanding about the concepts of educational school choice. Even respondents in cities such as Milwaukee and Cleveland where school choice programs using vouchers are already in place, know little more about these concepts than citizens in other parts of the United States (National Center for Policy Analysis, 2000). Adding to this confusion, the issue of school choice has become a hotly debated political topic. Proponents of school choice suggest it will reduce a school's tendency toward the bureaucratic. Some parents see it as an opportunity to take their children out of a school where they are unhappy or perhaps not successful. Some reformers feel that accountability, responsiveness, and quality will increase if the market mentality is applied to the school business. Opponents fear that school choice will jeopardize the long-cherished ideal of offering every child equal access to quality public schooling. Many educators harbor a sense of fear and distrust for any educational system outside the traditional public school. They argue that the free market just is not applicable to our school system (Choice and Vouchers, 2000). Certainly, these are important issues. But, while school boards, legislators, educators, and parents, in general, seek out the best answers to these concerns, we must not forget what education is all about. Ultimately, for parents and educators, the prevailing question must be "what is best for our children?" In the long run, "What is best for our children?" will be "What is best for our world?"

John, Che, Sonia, Tom, and Kim are typical children. Something was missing in their education. The fact that these young people needed something other than their traditional neighborhood school did not mean the public school had failed them. It just meant that at this point in time, these children had needs that, for whatever reason, were not being met. They needed something different. Educational school choice gave them the freedom to find a new school and a renewed opportunity to find success at school.

School Choice Options We Should Know About

Americans have many questions about school choice that need answers. How are schools of choice alike? How are they different? How are they financed?

Can any child attend a public magnet school? If children attend a charter school, how do we know that they are learning what they should be learning? Do state regulations govern private schools? If a parent decides to home-school a child, will that child be able to go to college? Are vouchers constitu-tional? What is a for-profit school? How do tax credits work? Is it true that if a child makes one mistake, he or she will be kicked out of a private school? Do public alternative schools only serve children who are discipline problems? Will only the best children go to choice schools? As an educator, will I earn credit toward retirement if I work in a choice school? If I send my child to a choice school or if I choose to work in a choice school, what will happen to our traditional, neighborhood public schools? What impact will this have on the neighborhood?

Parents who want the best for their children should not be criticized for considering a school of choice. Educators who consider which school would be the best place to work should not be criticized for opting to work in a school of choice. Neither should school of choice options be considered lightly without careful evaluation. Instead the opportunity for educational choice should be celebrated and supported as fundamental to a democratic society. But, in order to make informed educational choices that are best for children, all of us must become knowledgeable about the kinds of schools and issues represented in the school choice debate.

The chapters that follow will discuss many of the school choice options available in America today. In the first section, Chapter One focuses on what our Constitution says about educating America's children, and on important court cases that give definition to the issue of school choice. Chapters two through nine are categorized in two sections. Section two (chapters two through five) highlights public schools of choice, which include charter schools, magnet schools, alternative schools, and Educational Management Organizations (EMOs). Section three (chapters six through nine) focuses on private schools of choice and includes chapters on independent schools, Catholic schools, Christian schools, and homeschools. Each of section three's chapters begins with a general description of the type of school and discusses its structure and the legislative issues that apply. Other chapter topics include financing, accountability, and advantages and disadvantages. A list of Internet resources is available at the end of each chapter. The final section of this book, section four, summarizes elements of a caring school and focuses on what to look for in choosing a school for a child, or a school in which to teach.

Chapter References

Bomotti, S., Ginsberg, R., & Cobb, B. (1999). Teachers in charter schools and traditional schools: A comparative study. *Educational policy analysis*,7(22). [Online]. Available: *http://epaa.asu.edu/epaa/v7n22.html.*

Choice and Vouchers (2000). *Education Week.* [Online]. Available: *http://www .edweek.org/context/topics/choicea.htm.*

Finn, C. Manno, B., & Bierlein, L. (1996). *Charter schools in action: What have we learned? First-year report.* Washington, DC: Hudson Institute.

Harris, S. (2001). *A study of educators who choose to work in schools of choice.* Paper presented at the American Education Research Association annual conference. Seattle, Washington.

Hawkins, D. (1996, Feb.) *Home school battles. U.S. News & World Report,* 57–58.

National Center for Policy Analysis (2000). [Online]. Available: *http://www.ncpa .org/pi/edu/july98c.html.*

Olson, L. (2000, April 26). Redefining "public" schools. *Education Week.* [Online].A vailable: *http://www.edweek.org/ew/ew_printstory.cfm?slug+33na.h10.*

Public Agenda. (1999). *On thin ice: How advocates and opponents could misread the public's views on vouchers and charter schools.* Charles A. Dana Foundation. [Online]. Available: *http://www.publicagenda.org.*

Chapter One

Legal Aspects of School Choice Issues

Sandra Lowery, Ed.D.

The Tenth Amendment to the Constitution of the United States specifies that all powers not delegated to the federal government are delegated to the states. Since the Constitution of the United States does not address education, education is considered to be a responsibility of the states. Although education is a function of the 50 states, interpretations of the Bill of Rights and the First and Fourteenth Amendments to the U.S. Constitution in a number of court cases have directly impacted education. Additionally, federal legislation through grants, such as the National Defense Act, have had a significant influence.

Just as public education is a responsibility of the states, so are school choice issues. A variety of legal concerns pertaining to school choice decisions have been resolved through state and national courts. Court cases dealing with parental rights, compulsory attendance in public schools, governmental regulation of private schools, utilization of public funds for private schools, financial assistance to students and parents, and vouchers have provided resolution on these topics.

The Right to Direct a Child's Education

The courts have long upheld parental rights to direct the upbringing of children, including their education (McCarthy, Cambron-McCabe, & Thomas, 1998). Referring to earlier cases involving parental rights, Justice Sandra Day O'Connor (2000) said in a main opinion that "it cannot now be doubted that the due process clause of the 14th Amendment protects the fundamental rights of parents to make decisions concerning the care, custody, and control of their children."

In 1923, the constitutional right of parents to direct the education of their children was confirmed by the U.S. Supreme Court (*Meyer v. Nebraska*, 1923).

Strongly affirming parental rights in this case, the Court ruled that the authority to direct the upbringing and education of their children was a constitutionally protected right under the Fourteenth Amendment.

In a similar vein, a 1925 case—*Pierce v. Society of the Sisters*—decided by the U.S. Supreme Court provided constitutional protection to private schools' rights to exist and validated parental authority to choose private school education for their children as an alternative to public schooling (*Pierce v. Society of the Sisters*, 1925). In this case, the court also noted that the state has an interest in mandating school attendance and regulating private education for the purpose of ensuring educated citizens.

In a recent ruling, the U.S. Supreme Court once again strongly upheld the constitutional right of parents to control the upbringing of their children (*Troxel v. Granville*, 2000). In this strong pronouncement of parental rights, the Court ruled that parents have a fundamental authority, protected by the U.S. Constitution, to control the rearing of their children, including their education (Walsh, 2000). Court decisions spanning almost 80 years have reaffirmed parental rights, and these Court rulings have consistently been interpreted to include educational matters.

Compulsory Attendance

The issue of compulsory attendance has been litigated in a number of cases. The U.S. Supreme Court ruled that public schools may release students for religious instruction off public school grounds (*Zorach v. Clauson*, 1952). In a later case, the rights of parents who chose to send their children away from the public school one hour each week for religious instruction were upheld (*Smith v. Smith*, 1976). The issue of release time for religious instruction was considered in *McCollum v. Board of Education*, a case in which the U.S. Supreme Court ruled against the practice of using public school facilities for religious training conducted by clergy during the school day (*McCollum v. Board of Education*, 1948).

Although the courts have upheld the right for students to request and be granted time away from school to attend religious activities (*Johnson v. Charles City Community Schools Board of Education*, 1985), the judiciary has not condoned excessive absences for religious reasons (*Commonwealth v. Bey*, 1950).

In a landmark case that addressed compulsory attendance (*Wisconsin v. Yoder*, 1972), the courts provided a judicially approved exception to a state compulsory attendance law. In this case, Amish children were allowed to exit the public school system after completion of the eighth grade, due to the beliefs and lifestyles of the Amish.

The recent acceptance of homeschooling by the courts has put the question of compulsory attendance in a different perspective (*Johnson v. Charles City Community Schools Board of Education*, 1985). In recent years, state legislatures have changed compulsory attendance laws to provide for homeschooling. The degree of acceptance for homeschooling is illustrated in a report of the Home School Legal Defense Association. In 1982, only two states had legislation allowing homeschooling, but by 1996, that number had increased to 35 (Klicka, 1998).

State and Federal Regulation of Private Schools

Courts in several states, including the Ohio Supreme Court and the Kentucky Supreme Court, have struck down state regulations applied to private schools (McCarthy, Cambron-McCabe, & Thomas, 1998). Other state courts have ruled differently, upholding minimum state requirements and state regulation authority in Hawaii, Iowa, Michigan, Nebraska, North Dakota, and Vermont (McCarthy, Cambron-McCabe, & Thomas, 1998). Although homeschools enjoy great freedom, the courts generally have ruled that parents must comply with homeschooling regulations (*Battles v. Anne Arundel County Board of Education*, 1995).

The courts have held that private schools are responsible for compliance with state and federal employment laws, including those based on race, gender, and age. In fact, in one case, the U.S. Supreme Court ruled that the governmental interest in prohibiting racial discrimination was greater than the schools' right as a private institution (*Bob Jones University v. United States*, 1983).

Utilization of Public Funds for Private Schools

The First Amendment of the United States Constitution prohibits Congress from making laws that either respect establishment of religion or prohibit the free exercise of religion. This wall of separation philosophy has been predominant since it was stated in *Everson v. Board of Education* (*Everson v. Board of Education*, 1947). Although the First Amendment speaks specifically about

Congress, courts have ruled that it also applies to local and state governments, including school boards.

Despite the wall of separation between government and private schools, some state governments have enacted legislation that provides some tax funds for use by nonpublic schools (Burrup, Brimley, & Garfield, 1999). While the courts, including the U.S. Supreme Court, have not allowed direct state financial support of nonpublic schools, they have allowed Congress and state legislatures to provide some types of support, such as state income tax deductions in Minnesota (Kemerer, 1998) and tax credits in Illinois (Ryan, 1999).

Governmental support has been ruled admissible as long as it is not in violation of the Lemon Test. This test, used for many years to determine the constitutionality of practices challenged as religious activities, is widely accepted. An activity of a governmental entity, which is challenged as being in violation of the Establishment Clause of the U.S. Constitution, will be found to be constitutional if it complies with the three-prong test:

1. There is a legitimate, secular, nonreligious purpose for the activity;

2. The primary effect of the activity neither advances nor hinders religious belief or practice; and

3. The activity does not foster excessive entanglement between the governmental entity and religious concerns (*Lemon v. Kurtzman*, 1971).

The Child-Benefit Theory

Several types of public funding that directly benefit students, rather than the private educational institutions attended by those students, have been approved by the courts. This practice is commonly referred to as the child-benefit doctrine and it can be traced back to the case that upheld use of public funds for transportation of private school students and at the same time defined the wall of separation philosophy (*Everson v. Board of Education*, 1947). The rationale promoted by the child-benefit theory is that the children, not the private schools they represented, were the beneficiaries of funds. An educated citizenry has been argued to have both private and public benefits, providing economic benefits to both those individuals and society (Smith, 1952).

The National Defense Act (NDA) and Titles One and Two of the Education Consolidation Act of 1965 are examples of federal legislation providing funding to nonpublic educational institutions under the child-benefit theory. Title One funds may be used to provide educational services for educationally disadvantaged students in nonpublic schools, with the responsibility for administering the programs delegated to public school systems. Remedial reading, remedial mathematics, counseling, health services, and other instructional programs are designed to provide extra educational services to students who are failing or are most at risk of failing to meet student performance standards in schools with high concentrations of children from low-income families.

Title Two of the NDA provides funds to local educational agencies for the acquisition and use of instructional and educational materials, including library services and materials for elementary and secondary school students (*School Law Bulletin*, 2000). These programs are available for both public and nonprofit private schools, with the restriction that private schools utilize the funds in a manner that is secular, neutral, and nonideological, in accordance with the Lemon Test. This practice was recently upheld by the U.S. Supreme Court in a ruling that allowed private schools to own materials, equipment, and/or property purchased with Title Two funds (*Mitchell v. Helms*, 2000).

The Education and Consolidation and Improvement Act of 1981 and the Improving America's Act of 1994 have also provided federal funds to public school districts that benefit students in private schools under the Child Benefit provision. Both these acts provide funds that flow through public schools to the private schools (Burrup, Brimley, & Garfield, 1999).

Financial Assistance to Students and Parents

Financial assistance in the form of state income tax deductions has been found constitutional by the U.S. Supreme Court (Kemerer, 1998). In 1983, the Court upheld a Minnesota law that allowed state income tax deductions for expenses incurred in either public or private schooling. Expenses approved for income tax deduction included tuition, textbooks, and transportation (*Mueller v. Allen*, 1983). This decision stated that the state of Minnesota's decision to defray costs of education, regardless of the schools attended, had a purpose that was both secular and understandable.

Legislation in 1999 by the Illinois legislature allowing tax credit for parents who incur certain educational expenses for their children in K–12 public or private schools was described as an economic benefit to taxpayers by Illinois Governor George Ryan. Ryan also noted that there are savings for parents who spend on private schools and that other taxpayers benefit also because the costs of educating those children in public schools would be extensive (Ryan, 1999). Currently, only Iowa, Minnesota, Ohio, Illinois, and Rhode Island provide some type of tax benefit to parents of nonpublic school children (*School Law Bulletin*, 2000). Other cases have followed, building upon the Mueller decision.

In a unanimous decision, the U.S. Supreme Court ruled that the Establishment Clause of the U.S. Constitution did not prevent the provision of vocational rehabilitation services to a blind student who studied for the ministry at a Christian college (*Witters v. Washington Department of Services*, 1986). In this case, the Court noted that aid was given to the student who could then pass it along to the public or private institution of his choice.

Another case sanctioned services to a deaf student enrolled in a Catholic school. This student required a sign language interpreter under the provisions of the Individuals with Disabilities Education Act (*Zobrest v. Catalina Foothills School District*, 1993). The Court emphasized that the student, not the parochial school, was the beneficiary.

Vouchers

Proponents of government funded vouchers to pay private school tuition have argued that vouchers provide poor families, particularly those living in inner cities and attending poorly performing public schools, the opportunity of educational choice that have been available to more affluent families (Metcalf & Tait, 1999). Voucher supporters have also maintained that giving parents more options in choosing schools will increase competition and force public schools to improve and that private schools are not mired in the bureaucracy and regulations that hamstring public schools (WestEd, 2000). During his campaign for the presidency, President George W. Bush supported a plan that included $1,500 vouchers that students in consistently failing schools could trade for private school tuition (Cobb, 2001).

Opponents of vouchers have argued that vouchers will not substantially improve public schools and that only a relatively small group of students will benefit from vouchers (Ramirez, 1998). Other critics of vouchers have noted that vouchers will weaken the public school system, draining financial resources (WestEd, 2000). Despite President Bush's support, Congress in the Spring 2001 session did not support any voucher plan in the education bill that was passed.

The U.S. Supreme Court has allowed a 1999 Wisconsin Supreme Court ruling, *Jackson v. Benson*, to stand. In this case, up to 15% of the students in the Milwaukee Public Schools are allowed to attend private schools (including religious schools), with the state paying tuition costs (Underwood, 1999).

More recently, the sixth U.S. Circuit Court of Appeals ruled that a voucher program involving nearly 4,000 students who are using tax-paid vouchers to pay private school tuition in Cleveland, Ohio, can continue to operate while supporters seek review by the U.S. Supreme Court (Cobb, 2001). The constitutionality of spending public funds on private schools, particularly on religious schools, is an especially strong debate that will likely be finally resolved only by the highest court in the nation, the U.S. Supreme Court.

Summary

Enrollments at public elementary and secondary schools in the United States are expected to grow by 1.3 million students in the next five years (Reinvigorating Our Schools, 2000). This increase in enrollment is expected to increase the need for a variety of schooling options for children (Marx, 2001). School choice debates and issues are likely to continue, with resolution in the court systems at local, state, and national levels. As significant societal changes are taking place at local, national, and global levels, challenges to traditionally held ideas about schooling are sure to follow.

Additional Resources:

The following Web sites provide general information about school choice issues:

- *http://www.edreform.com/pubs/stysts97.htm*
  Center for Educational Reform

- *http://www.uscharterschools.org/cs/uscsp/query/q/121?xxtitle=Guidance+on+Federal+Programs*
  Charter schools

- *http://www.tea.state.tx.us/charter/faq.html*
  Texas Education Agency

- *http://www.tasb.org/tcer/reports/update.html#Finance+Equity*
  Texas Association of School Boards

- *http://www.tasb.org/tcer/reports/update.jhtml#*
  Expansion of public school choice

Chapter References

Burrup, P., Brimley, V., & Garfield, R. (1999). *Financing education in a climate of change* (7th ed.). Boston: Allyn & Bacon.

Cobb, K. (2001, March 25). School vouchers continue in Ohio amid uncertainty. *Houston Chronicle*, pp. A10–A11.

Kemerer, F. (1998). The constitutional dimension of school vouchers. *Texas Forum on Civil Liberties & Civil Rights*, 3 (2), 158–161.

Klicka, C. J. (1998). Home schooling in the United States: a legal analysis. Paconian Springs, VA: Home School Legal Defense Association. In M. McCarthy, N. Cambron-McCabe, & S. Thomas (Eds.). *Public school law: Teachers' and students' rights* (4th ed.). Boston: Allyn & Bacon.

Marx, G. (2001). *Ten trends: Educating children for a profoundly different culture.* Arlington, VA: Educational Research Service.

McCarthy, M., Cambron-McCabe, N., & Thomas, S. (1998). *Public school law: teachers' and students' rights* (4th ed.). Boston: Allyn & Bacon.

Metcalf, K., Tait, P. (1999). Free market policies and public education: What is the cost of choice? *Phi Delta Kappan*, 81 (1). [Online]. Available: *http://www.pdkintl.org/kappan/kmet9909.htm.*

O'Connor, S. (2000) In Court affirms rights of parents to control children's upbringing. *Education Week.* [Online]. Available: *http://www.edweek.com/ew/ew_printstory.cfm.*

Ramirez, A. (1998). Vouchers and voodoo economics. *Educational Leadership*, 56 (2), 33–39.

Reinvigorating our schools (2000). *American Institute of Architects.* [Online]. Available: *http://www.e-architect.com/resources/schools/home2.asp.*

Ryan, G. (1999). In Illinois legislature approves education tax credit. *What's New Council for American Private Education.* [Online]. Available: *http://www.capenet.org/new.html.*

School Law Bulletin (2000, August). Vol. 27, No. 7.

Smith, A. (1952). An inquiry into the nature and causes of the wealth of nations. In R. M. Hutchins & M. J. Adler (Eds.): *Great books of the western world.* Vol. 39. Chicago: Encyclopedia Britannica.

Underwood, J. (1999). Vouchers—a legal draw. *American School Board Journal.* [Online]. Available: *http://www.tasanet.org/EducatorsJobBank/ejb.html.*

Walsh, M. (2000). Court affirms rights of parents to control children's upbringing. *Education Week.* [Online]. Available: *http://www.edweek.com/ew/ew_printstory.cfm.*

WestEd, U.S. Department of Education, Western Regional Laboratory. (2000). *What we know about vouchers: The facts behind the rhetoric.* San Francisco, CA: WestEd.

Court Cases

Battles v. Anne Arundel County Board of Education, 904 F. Supp. 471 (1995).

Bob Jones University v. United States, 461 U.S. 574, 592 (1983).

Commonwealth v. Bey, 70 A. 2d 693 (Pa. Super. Ct. 1950).

Everson v. Board of Education (1947).

Jackson v. Benson, Wisconsin (1999).

Johnson v. Charles City Community Schools Board of Education, 368 N.W. 2d 74 (Iowa 1985).

Lemon v. Kurtzman, 403 U.S. 602, 91S.Ct. 2105 (1971).

McCollum v. Board of Education, 333 U.S. 203 (1948).

Meyer v. Nebraska, 22 U.S. 390 (1923).

Mitchell v. Helms, 98–1648 U.S. (2000).

Mueller v. Allen, 463 U.S. 388 (1983).

Pierce v. Society of the Sisters, 268 U.S. 510, 45 S. Ct. 571, 69 L.Ed. 1070 (1925).

Smith v. Smith, 523 F.2d. 121 (4th Cir. 1975), cert. Denied, 423 U.S. 1073 (1976).

Troxel v. Granville, 99-138, U.S. (2000).

Wisconsin v. Yoder, 406 U.S. 205 (1972).

Witters v. Washington Department of Services, 474 U.S. 481, 1986.

Zobrest v. Catalina Foothills School District, 509 U.S., 1993.

Zorach v. Clauson, 343 U.S. 306 (1952)

Section Two

Public Schools of Choice

Sandra Harris, Ph.D.

In the mid-1800s, Horace Mann, frequently called "the father of American education," considered education the key to the "reform of society" (Spring, 1996, p. 9). It was his dream that all children would attend a school "common to all children" to share in a "common education" (p. 9). However, because of economic, cultural, and societal differences and the influence on where children live, American education "has never really been common to all children" (p. 10). Typically, the public schools in America have assigned children to the local neighborhood school based on the residence of the child. Thus, until the 1970s, the only opportunity that parents had to choose for their child a school that was not in their attendance zone was to move to another location, unless they were able to afford a private school.

In the battle against school desegregation, public magnet schools were first created in the 1970s to provide educational opportunities for black children to integrate schools. While integrating schools is still the main legal imperative and justification, magnet schools of today include themed schools within schools and career academies.

The first public charter schools opened in the early 1990s and are now the fastest growing public school of choice. Charter schools operate with considerable autonomy and independence. These schools frequently serve specialized populations, such as the learning disabled or other students considered to be at risk.

Academic alternative schools offer opportunities for students that can include, among other things, graduating early from high school by choosing individualized curricula. These schools, an integral part of a local school district, are open to all students living within the district, and, occasionally, even to those who live outside the district.

Educational management organizations (EMOs) are for-profit schools that provide school management and instructional services. School districts contract with EMOs to provide management and instruction to specific schools within the district. Some charter schools are also funded by EMOs.

Most of the public school districts in the United States receive almost 50% of their financial support from local taxes, thus, children who attend school in wealthy areas have more money spent on their education than children attending schools with little taxable wealth (Spring, 1996). Public school choice opportunities that include magnet schools, charter schools, alternative schools, and EMOs are an effort by public schools to reduce the inequalities in American education. In the chapters that follow, these public educational opportunities are considered to expand Horace Mann's dream for a common education to mean that all children in American have "in common" the opportunity for an extension of schooling options.

Reference

Spring, J. (1996). *American education* (7th ed.) New York: McGraw-Hill, Inc.

Chapter Two

Magnet Schools

Raymond A. Horn, Jr., Ph.D.

Introduction

Throughout the 20th century ideological and economic forces struggled to control American education. At various times the purpose of education was to supply industry with trained workers, to solve social problems through the education of children, to promote the development of a citizen who would democratically participate in American society, or to meet the unique developmental needs of every child. As this struggle continued through the century, parents had little input into the purpose of their *own* child's education. As educational trends affected curriculum, instruction, assessment, and the organization of the school, parental beliefs about the purpose of education and their children's unique and personal needs were subordinate to those of the politicians, industrialists, and educators. Of course, private schools always were an option for some parents; however, this option was limited by the focus of the schools and the tuition and transportation costs to the parents.

In the 1970s, another possibility emerged that provided new options for parents who were dissatisfied with their local public school. This option would grow to include over 1.5 million students in America (Black, 1996). Depending on the school offerings, parents could choose to have their children:

- learn their lessons in French or Spanish, as 425 students do in an elementary school in Greenville, South Carolina (Black, 1996);

- attend a public Montessori school at no additional expense (School District of Palm Beach County, 2001);

- choose between nine elementary schools with themes ranging from the world of plants and animals, working with people of different cultures, learning in a mini-market society, experiencing a hands-on approach to math and science, to learning in a school dedicated to the performing and visual arts (Roanoke City Magnet Schools, 2001);

- participate in a school devoted to the development of early childhood literacy (Crowell, Crites, & Wortman, 1991);

- remain in their own school but explore the world with experts in any field through a "virtual" magnet school (Goodrich, 1994);

- be part of a middle-school magnet program for gifted students (Juntune, 1999);

- or, in Phoenix, Arizona if the parents are homeless, they can enroll their children in a school that meets the unique needs of transient children (Woods & Harrison, 1994).

The inclusion of choice within some public school districts has proven to be so successful that "more than 60 percent of magnet schools cannot accommodate all the students who wish to enroll, and about half of all magnet programs maintain waiting lists. Upwards of 120,000 students are on those lists" (Black, 1996, p. 35). Magnet schools have become so successful that "many parents would send their children to private schools if it were not for the magnet schools and some parents remove their children from private schools once they are accepted into a magnet program" (Algozzine, Yon, Nesbit, & Nesbit, 1999, p. 182). The appeal to parents as seen through the growth of magnet schools supports the continuing trend "that parents should be able to choose schools, that the education system should provide more educational options, and that schools should be accountable through market forces" (Archibald, 1996, p. 152).

Magnet School History and Legislation

The original and primary purpose of magnet schools was "to reduce racial isolation by attracting students to a desegregated setting" (Met, 1993, p. 71). In 1954, *Brown v. Board of Education* began the desegregation of American schools. In the 1960s this desegregation effort was characterized by court ordered busing. One result of this busing was "white flight" to the suburbs and white parents moving their children to private and/or religious schools. "Unless attractive options were found within public schools systems, many feared that 'white flight' would defeat desegregation plans" (Taylor & Yu, 1999, p. 15). President Richard Nixon addressed this white parental reaction by introducing a mechanism of choice into the desegregation movement (Meeks, Meeks, & Warren, 2000). In 1971, the Supreme Court agreed in their decision *Swann v. Charlotte-Mecklenburg Board of Education* that a diversity of techniques including quotas, transportation, pairing schools, and designing new attendance zones could be used to achieve racial balance (Goldberg, 1988). In 1976, Congress passed the Emergency School Aid Act (ESAA), which "attempted to 'pluralize' educational offerings in an effort to encourage voluntary desegregation of our nation's school districts through a magnet concept" (Hardin, 1983).

The ESAA provided federal financial aid in "ending minority isolation and improving the quality of education for everyone" (Hardin, 1983, p. 48). The use of magnet schools as desegregation tools grew rapidly from 1976 to 1981 as federal funding increased from $10 million to $40 million during this period (Hardin, 1983). President Ronald Reagan continued the magnet school desegregation effort through the Magnet School Assistance Program, in which between 1985 and 1993 the federal government spent $739 million in promoting magnet schools (Steele & Eaton, 1996).

However, the purpose of the magnet school concept quickly evolved to include other purposes, such as:

- promoting greater curricular and instructional choices in the attempt to satisfy parents' interests and priorities (Blank & Archibald, 1992; Douzenis, 1994; Hardin, 1983; Morris & Goldring, 1999; Smrekar & Goldring, 1999);

- improving scholastic standards and providing high quality education in urban schools (Clinchy, 1985; Goldring & Smrekar, 2000; Lezotte & Taylor, 1989);

- renewing interest and motivation of teachers (Clinchy, 1985);

- improving a school system's image in the community (Clinchy, 1985);

- developing a sense of community (Smrekar & Goldring, 1999);

- providing an opportunity for educational innovation (Farmer & Farmer, 2000)

The diversity of purpose is clear in the Web site statement of the purpose of the Palm Beach County School District's magnet programs: expand educational choices for students; set high expectations for all students to achieve academically; promote diversity within our schools; meet the interests and needs of students; enhance parent/community involvement; prepare students for further education and/or careers in the world of work; provide field-based and hands-on learning experiences; and offer mentorship, internship, and apprenticeship opportunities (School District of Palm Beach County, 2001).

Another purpose has to do with the shift from centralized to decentralized student assignment (Archibald, 1996; Clincy, 1998; Lee, 1993). The centralized assignment system is the traditional practice of assigning students to schools within their own neighborhood school zone. Under the decentralized model the neighborhood boundaries are deemphasized and parents are allowed to determine the school that their child will attend. The decentralized model provides advantages such as: "schools can specialize in particular ways: curriculum programs, educational philosophies, technologies, teaching methods, organizational structures, etc. Schools can be designed to accommodate parent work schedules, day care needs, or other types of needs. In the school choice model, sameness is the problem, not the solution" (Archibald, 1996, p. 152). Decentralized schools can attract parents from a wide geographical area because of content specialization or because of a particular pedagogical style, such as open, basics, Montessori, or extended day (Farmer & Farmer, 2000; Raywid, 1984).

An additional purpose of magnet schools is to promote the open marketplace concept of education. This concept proposes "that public education has become a monopoly that is wasteful, overregulated, unresponsive to captive clients, and shockingly inefficient" (Tyack, 1992, p. 14). The assumption is made that by providing competition between schools the number of efficient schools will increase. In this model, parents and students are viewed "as clients or customers and schools as businesses, solely responsible for their own quality" (Archibald, 1996, p. 153). The marketplace model of choice views education as a consumer good. However, regardless of the purpose of magnet schools, the organizational diversity of magnet schools challenges traditional education.

Structure

As previously mentioned, magnet schools can be organized around content themes, instructional techniques, or the special needs of students. Whatever the organizational structure, all magnet schools offer a complete curriculum in addition to their specialization. "The magnet school is one that students attend full-time for all of their courses, and one in which all students are magnet students. The advantage of this model is that it provides for more concentration of resources. The disadvantage is the isolation of the students from the mainstream" (Von Seggern, 1990, p. 51).

Another organizational option is the "magnet program within schools" model. "In this model, students attend other classes with the regular school population and attend magnet theme classes for intensive instruction" (Von Seggern, 1990, p. 51). In some cases, students are bused from their home school to a center for one day a week or for part of a day. Some schools integrate the magnet program within the regular program (Juntune, 1999). This is one way to offset the criticism that the regular student population suffers when certain types of students leave the school (Archibald, 1996; Von Seggern, 1990). This organizational model lessens the impact of the magnet program on the regular program, and further addresses the criticism that magnet schools promote elitism.

Concerning the selection of students for the magnet schools, the fundamental component of the selection process is that parents volunteer for the school or self-select the school. This volunteerism is regulated to ensure a population diversity that represents a wide range of cultural, socioeconomic, and linguistic backgrounds (Crowell, Crites, & Wortman, 1991). Other selection components could include required test scores, good grades, recommendations, and preference if a student already has siblings in the school. Generally, selection is done on a "first come, first served process"; however, lotteries are used if there are more students than vacancies. Lotteries are generally computerized to maintain a balance between all neighborhoods within the school's attendance area, gender, race, and ethnicity (Lezotte, 1989; School District of Palm Beach County, 2001; Thacker, 1997). In some cases, a "weighted" lottery is used to assign extra weight to various applicants based on various factors (Roanoke City Magnet Schools, 2001).

Finances

The parents of children who are selected do not have to pay extra fees. Since magnet schools are public schools, owned and operated by school districts (Jones, 1998, p. 3), there are no additional tuition fees, user fees, or transportation fees. In fact, expenditures per student run 10% higher in many districts with magnets (Goldring & Smrekar, 2000). Additional funds are secured through partnerships between the schools and local industry. An excellent example of partnerships occurs in Atlanta, Georgia, in which numerous businesses provide additional support for all of the magnet schools (Fraser, 1986).

Accountability

Magnet schools are held to the same accountability procedures and protocols as any other public school in their state. If their state has a standards and accountability system that includes a high-stakes exit level test, the magnet school students must perform to the same level as the other public school students. In states that allow more local control over curriculum and instruction, magnets only have to answer to the local school board. This allows the organizational structure of magnet schools to vary from the traditional school structures. In addition, "magnet schools operate in much the same way neighborhood public schools do with regard to teacher certification, unionism and school rules of student conduct. All teachers must meet the same certification requirements as those in neighborhood schools. Union membership and work rules apply in magnet schools as in other public schools" (Jones, 1998, p. 4).

Advantages and Disadvantages

Does educational effectiveness follow organizational innovation? Proponents of magnet schools cite three basic reasons for any educational effectiveness in these schools: choice, commitment, and the ability of the schools to control who attends the school (Doyle & Levine, 1984). These reasons are supposed to lead to improved learning, high morale, and a heightened sense of community. Other factors involve strong administrative leadership, a sense of mission, clear instructional focus, high expectations, use of student achievement data for remediation, a safe and orderly environment, and parental involvement (Thacker, 1997).

Myriam Met (1993) proposes that magnet schools have greatly affected second language learning by increasing immersion programs in magnet schools from 1 to 67 in the last 20 years. Another benefit of magnet schools is that students in magnet schools significantly outperform other students and are twice as likely to finish high school (Black, 1996). A minority school district in Maryland reported magnet school student achievement surpassing that of other schools by 10% in language, 6 percent in mathematics, and 8% in reading (Lyons & Walton, 1988). Larger studies have also found that magnet students generally have the highest performance (Archibald, 1995; Blank, 1989; Gamoran, 1996a, 1996b; Heebener, 1995).

Critics of magnet schools attribute the higher academic performance to other factors. One criticism is that this higher performance is due to the creation of a dual school system, in which the "cream" is "skimmed" off the top, resulting in a segregation of able and less able students (Archibald, 1996). This "creaming" effect keeps middle-class students in the urban system but also retracts the schools—in other words, it creates a two-tracked or two-tiered educational system (Carlson, 1999; Hill, Foster, & Gendler, 1990; Thornton & Chunn, 1987–1988). Despite the self-selection process, creaming also occurs because many low-income families do not have the information, time, and access to transportation to make the necessary contact with the school (Hawley, 1996; Moore & Davenport, 1989); Morris & Goldring, 1999).

Boundaries created by race and socioeconomic class still exist in some magnet schools because poorer and minority parents do not have equitable access to the information about the selection process and the school (Archibald, 1996; Yon, Nesbit, & Algozzine, 1998). In addition, the criticism that magnet schools foster elitism and socioeconomic segregation is supported in that the parents of many magnet schools have higher income and education levels and are more likely to be employed than nonmagnet parents (Morris & Goldring, 1999; Slusher, 1986). In fact, in some areas, white families are still more likely to transfer to schools with low proportions of minorities and minority families opt for low-income neighborhoods (Henig, 1995).

Other criticisms include a concern about safety issues involving bus riders, the curtailment of after-school activities, and the deleterious effect of magnet schools on neighborhood communities not adjacent to the schools (Goldring & Smrekar, 2000; Smrekar, 1996). Critics of the marketplace model argue that all people, not just parents, should have a say about how to educate the young, and that the effectiveness of schools is reduced to a competition among schools to produce the best test scores (Tyack, 1992). Finally, critics point out that magnet school performance should be better when a school has the greatest resources, the most committed teachers, and the most educationally minded families. If all schools received 25 to 50% more funding, than all schools would show high student performance (Jones, 1998).

Summary

Are magnet schools more effective? The answer is unclear, specifically due to the highly contextual nature of the magnet school experience. In other words, the touted benefits can vary in many ways from school to school. In one school, parents are trained to use computers and can check out computers and books in order to become partners in their children's learning (Crowell et al. 1991). Obviously, strategies like this create the potential for higher student performance. Also, the simple fact is that "magnet schools do openly what affluent neighborhood and suburban schools do unofficially" (Metz, 1988, p. 57).

Therefore, parents need to research carefully the specific school that might serve their children. The following are basic questions that can allow parents to make an informed decision about magnet schools:

- Who are the students who attend this program?

- What does the school prepare students to do?

- What is the nature and level of parental involvement in the school?

- How are teachers prepared for teaching in this program?

- What types of enrichment activities are offered?

Additional Resources

Most, if not all, magnet schools have a Web site that can be found through any search engine by using the keywords "magnet schools."

- *http://www.magnet.edu*

- *http://www.magnetschool.com*

- *http://www.edunet.ie/links/magnet.html*
  Directory of magnet schools in the United States

- *http://web66.coled.umn.edu/schools/lists/science.html*
  Directory of science magnet schools

- *http://www.ksg.harvard.edu/pepg/papers.htm*
  School choice in general

- *http://www.goodschools.gwu.edu/*
  School reform in general

- *http://www.schoolreformers.com*
  School reform in general

- *http://eric-web.tc.columbia.edu/digests/dig76.html*
  Eric Clearinghouse on Urban Education

Chapter References

Algozzine, B., Yon, M., Nesbit, C., & Nesbit, J. (1999). Parent perceptions of a magnet school program. *Journal of Research and Development in Education, 32* (3), 178–183).

Archibald, D. (1995). A longitudinal cohort analysis of achievement among elementary-magnet students, neighborhood-school students and transfer students. *Journal of Research and Development in Education,* 28 (3), 161–168.

Archibald, D. (1996). SES and demographic predictors of magnet school enrollment. *Journal of Research and Development in Education,* 29 (3), 152–162.

Black, S. (1996). The pull of magnets. *The American School Board Journal,* 183 (9), 34–36.

Blank, R. F. (1989). *Educational effects of magnet high schools.* Madison: National Center on Effective Secondary Schools, University of Wisconsin–Madison.

Blank, R. K., & Archibald, D. A. (1992). Magnet schools and issues of education quality. *Clearing House,* 66 (2), 81–86.

Carlson, D. (1999). The rules of the game: Detracking and retracking the urban high school. In F. Yeo, & B. Kanpol (Eds.), *From nihilism to possibility: Democratic transformations for the inner city* (pp. 15–36). Cresskill, NJ: Hampton Press.

Clinchy, E. (1985). Let magnet schools guide the way to education reform—and diversity. *American School Board Journal,* 172 (5), 43.

Clinchy, E. (1998). Democratizing America's public schools. *Principal,* 77 (5), 13–14, 16.

Crowell, C., Crites, A., & Wortman, B. (1991). Borton primary magnet school: Winner of IRA's 1991 exemplary reading program award. *Arizona Reading Journal,* 20 (1), 15–17.

Douzenis, C. (1994). Evaluation of magnet schools: Methodological issues and concerns. *Clearing House,* 68 (1), 15–18.

Doyle, D. P., & Levine, M. (1984). Magnet schools: Choice and quality in public education. *Phi Delta Kappan,* 66 (4), 265–270.

Farmer, B. W., & Farmer, E. I. (2000). Organizational structures of teachers in traditional and magnet schools in a large urban school district. *Education and Urban Society,* 33 (1), 60–73.

Fraser, L. A. (1986). Atlanta: Magnet schools discover the power of partnership. *ProEducation,* 3 (3), 33–34, 39.

Gamoran, A. (1996a). Student achievement in public magnet, public comprehensive, and private city high schools. *Educational Evaluation and Policy Analysis*, 18 (1), 1–18.

Gamoran, A. (1996b). Do magnet schools boost achievement? *Educational Leadership*, 54 (2), 42–46.

Goldberg, S. S. (1988). Book review: Different by design: The context and character of three magnet schools. *West's Education Law Reporter*, 48 (2), 329–332.

Goldring, E., & Smrekar, C. (2000). Magnet schools and the pursuit of racial balance. *Education and Urban Society*, 33 (1), 17–35.

Goodrich, B. E. (1994). Creating a "virtual" magnet school. *T.H.E. Journal* 21, (10), 73–75.

Hardin, T. L. (1983). The politics of pulling in and holding on: The magnet school concept in Kankakee, Illinois. *Illinois Schools Journal*, 63 (1–4), 48–56.

Hawley, W. D. (1996). The false premises and false promises of the movement to privatize education. In E. C. Lageman and L. P. Miller (Eds.), *Brown v. Board: The challenge for todays's schools* (pp. 135–142). New York: Teachers College Press.

Heebener, A. L. (1995). The impact of career magnet high schools: Experimental and qualitative evidence. *Journal of Vocational Education Research*, 20 (2), 27–55.

Henig, J. R. (1995). Race and choice in Montgomery County, Maryland, magnet schools. *Teachers College Record* (4), 729–734.

Hill, P. T., Foster, G. E., & Gendler, T. (1990). *High schools with character*. Santa Monica: The RAND Corporation.

Jones, T. H. (1998). Public school options: Magnet and charter schools. *School Business Affairs*, 6, 3–6, 8–12.

Juntune, J. E. (1999). Blending a middle school magnet program for gifted students with a regular middle school program. *NASSP Bulletin*, 83 (609), 96–102.

Lee, V. (1993). Educational choice: The stratifying effects of selecting schools and courses. *Educational Policy*, 7, 125–148.

Lezotte, L. W., & Taylor, B. O. (1989). How closely can magnet schools be aligned with the effective schools model? *Equity and Choice*, 5 (1), 25–29.

Lyons, J. E., & Walton, K. (1988). Magnetic attractions: Desegregating a minority school district. *Educational Record*, 68 (4), 32–34.

Meeks, L. F., Meeks, W. A., & Warren, C. A. (2000). Racial desegregation magnet schools, vouchers, privatization, and home schooling. *Education and Urban Society*, 33 (1), 88–101.

Met, M. (1993). Second language learning in magnet school contexts. *Annual Review of Applied Linguistics*, 13, 71–85.

Metz, M. H. (1988). In education, magnets attract controversy. *NEA Today: A Newspaper for Members of the National Education Association*, 6 (6), 54–60.

Moore, D., & Davenport, S. (1989). *The new improved sorting machine: Concerning school choice*. Chicago: Designs for Change.

Morris, J. E., & Goldring, E. (1999). Are magnet schools more equitable? An analysis of the disciplinary rates of african american and white students in Cincinnati magnet and nonmagnet schools. *Equity & Excellence in Education*, 32 (3), 59–65.

Raywid, M. A. (1984). Synthesis of research on schools of choice. *Educational Leadership*, 4 (7), 70–89.

Roanoke City Magnet Schools. (2001). *Magnet Schools*. [Online]. Available: *http://208.27.234.2/magnet/home.html*.

School District of Palm Beach County. (2001). *Magnet Schools and Programs* [Online]. Available: www.palmbeach.k12.fl.us/maps/tempmag/magnet.htm.

Slusher, J. (1986). Magnet schools attract, . . . but do they desegregate? *Youth Policy*, 8 (9), 10–12.

Smrekar, C. (1996). *The impact of school choice and community: In the interest of families and schools*. Albany: State University of New York Press.

Smrekar, C., & Goldring, E. B. (1999). *School choice in urban America: Magnet schools and the pursuit of equity*. New York: Teachers College Press.

Steele, L., & Eaton, M. (1996). *Reducing, eliminating, and preventing minority isolation in American schools: The impact of the Magnet Schools Assistance Program*. Washington, DC: American Institutes for Research.

Taylor, W. L., & Yu, C. M. (1999). The context of magnet schools: The policies and politics of desegregation in Cincinnati and St. Louis. In C. Smrekar & E. Goldring (Eds.), *School choice in urban America: Magnet schools and the pursuit of equity* (pp. 15–25). New York: Teachers College Press.

Thacker, J. L. (1997). Establishment of a new magnet school: Effects on student achievement. *ERS Spectrum*, 15 (1), 43–47.

Thornton, A., & Chunn, E. W. (1987–1988). Desegregating with magnet and one-race elementary and secondary schools. *The Urban League Review*, 11 (1–2), 146–157.

Tyack, D. (1992). Can we build a system of choice that is not just a "sorting machine" or a market-based "free for all"? *Equity and Choice*, 9 (1), 13–17.

Von Seggern, M. (1990). Magnet music programs: A look at the issues. *Music Educators Journal*, 76 (7), 50–53.

Woods, C. J. & Harrison, D. (1994). A magnet for homeless students: The Thomas J. Pappas Regional Education Center. *Clearing House*, 68 (2), 123–126

Yon, M., Nesbit, C., & Algozzine, B. (1998). Racial and social class isolation in magnet schools. *Journal of Research in Childhood Education*, 13 (1), 77–84.

Chapter Three

Charter Schools

Diane Porter Patrick, Ph.D.
Sandra Harris, Ph.D.

Although the charter school movement is a relatively new educational choice in the United States, public charter schools rapidly emerged as a viable educational option during the last decade of the 20th century. While the number of charter schools has increased each year, likewise the number of children educated in these schools has grown to the point that charter schools have become one of the most significant options in public schools of choice.

Charter schools are nonsectarian public schools that are publicly funded and controlled but typically operated more like private schools in a free market environment. Although charter schools receive government funding to operate, they are dependent on the satisfaction of their customers to stay in business because parents are free to choose their children's school. The school's charter is a performance contract with the granting authority that holds the school responsible for academic goals and fiscal practices.

Since the first 1991 charter legislation enacted in Minnesota, 36 states, plus the District of Columbia and Puerto Rico, have passed charter school laws, and this type of school reform is under consideration in approximately a dozen other states. Today approximately 2,000 publicly financed charter schools are operated relatively free from state and local regulations by a wide range of organizations from community groups to for-profit companies (The State of Charter Schools 2000, 2000; Charter School Legislation, 2000).

Some have suggested that the charter school movement may result in the ultimate organizational model for site-based decision making. As proposed in his book *Education by Charter: Restructuring School Districts* (1988), educator Ray Budde is considered by many to be the founder of the charter concept in the United States. He suggested, "It is the 'factory model' school district which needs to be replaced by a services-oriented infrastructure—and chartering *all* schools is a vehicle for making this happen" (R. Budde, personal communication, February 12, 1997).

Charter schools are created for many reasons. The primary motivation for starting a charter school is to provide a vision of schooling that was not realized in the traditional neighborhood public school. Because these schools are more autonomous than other schools, they have the freedom to use alternative curricula and nonstandardized approaches. They also have the opportunity to create a school with a shared vision. More and more, charter schools are being started to serve a specialized population. Approximately one in four charter schools are created to serve students often considered "at risk" (Manno, 2001).

As more charter schools have opened their doors each year, the number of the nation's public school students attending these schools is also increasing. The first charter school opened in St. Paul, Minnesota, with approximately 60 students, and as of the year 2000, California alone has over 120,000 students enrolled in charter schools, the most charter students of any state (Charter Schools in California, 2000).

Table 1 shows the explosive growth of charter schools nationwide during the five-year period from 1995 through 2000, at which point over 430,000 were enrolled in charter schools. The Washington-based Center for Education Reform (CER) estimated that over 500,000 children began the school year 2000 in more than 2,000 charter schools. To put these figures in perspective, however, the number of students attending charter schools amounts to less than 1% of the nation's 54 million public school students (The State of

---

Table 1
Charter School Growth from 1995–2000

Year	Schools	Students
1995–1996	223	21,664
1996–1997	500	100,000
1997–1998	700	170,000
1998–1999	1,050	252,000
1999–2000	1,674	430,000
2000–2001*	2,000	500,000

*estimate
Source: CER National Charter School Directory 2000 (2000). The Center for Education Reform. [Online]. Available: *http://www.edreform.com/press/nscd2000.htm.*

Charter Schools, 2000; *CER National Charter School Directory 2000*; Finn, Mano, & Bierlein, 1996; Vanourek, Manno, Finn, & Bierlein, 1997).

As indicated in Table 2, as of 1999, five states had over 100 charter schools in operation. With nearly 350 schools in operation, Arizona leads the nation in the number of charter schools. California ranks second with 234 schools, followed by Michigan with 175, Texas with 168, and Florida with 112 (*Overview of Charter Schools USCS*).

Table 2

Estimated Number of Charter Schools in Operation as of September 1999, by State

Year Law Passed	State	Number of Schools
1994	Arizona	348
1992	California	234
1994	Michigan	175
1995	Texas	168
1996	Florida	112
1996	North Carolina	83
1993	Colorado	68
1991	Minnesota	57
1995	New Jersey	52
1997	Ohio	48
1997	Pennsylvania	45
1993	Wisconsin	45
1993	Massachusetts	39
1993	Georgia	32
1996	District of Columbia	28
1996	Illinois	19
1995	Louisiana	17
1994	Kansas	15
1998	Missouri	14
1996	South Carolina	10
1998	Idaho	8
1998	Utah	8
1997	Nevada	5

continued

Year Law Passed	State	Number of Schools
1995	Delaware	5
1998	New York	3
1993	New Mexico	3
1995	Rhode Island	2
1994	Hawaii	2
1999	Oregon	1
1997	Mississippi	1
1999	Oklahoma	0
1998	Virginia	0
1995	New Hampshire	0
1995	Wyoming	0
1995	Arkansas	0
Total		1,682

Source: *Overview of Charter Schools* USCS. [Online]. Available: *http://www.uscharterschools.org/lpt/uscs _docs/58.*

However, serving an average of about 250 students, charter schools in general are smaller than most traditional schools. Furthermore, they are "organized in a variety of grade configurations from the entire span of kindergarten–grade 12 to various combinations such as elementary and middle school or middle and high school" (Patrick, 1997, p. 5).

Three ideologies appear to drive charter school growth: antibureaucracy, market-based, and teacher professionalism (Garn, 1998). The *antibureaucracy* ideology contends that educational innovation is being restricted by state education codes that do not allow opportunity for creative growth because they focus on top-down systems. For example, in Texas and in other states, charter schools are exempt from state statutes and rules that relate to schools, but they still must comply with federal and state statutes that involve health, safety, and civil rights (Taebel et al., 1997).

The second philosophy that undergirds the growth of charter schools is that of a *market-based* competition. Critics of the public school system insist that traditional public schools exist regardless of educational outcomes because they are able to monopolize the system (Garn, 1998). In other words, parents send their children to the local neighborhood public school because there is no alternative. Proponents of letting parents choose the schools their children attend think that a market approach to reform will foster healthy competition. Advocates assert that such competition can serve as a catalyst for innovative practices in traditional district schools. The result will be that poorly performing schools either will improve or go out of business (Chubb & Moe, 1990).

The third ideology fueling the charter school movement is that of *teacher professionalism.* Ideally in these schools, teacher expertise is valued and teachers are empowered, especially in the area of classroom instruction. Teachers, not administrators, would make and implement decisions that will have the greatest impact on student learning (Garn, 1998).

Charter School Structure

State charter laws specify whether the charter-granting authorities are local boards, state boards of education, or universities. Charters may be granted to teachers, parents, universities, community members, business leaders, and other interested groups (Patrick, 1997). Although charter contracts vary from state to state, they typically include these four components: (a) an instructional plan; (b) specific educational results and how they will be measured; (c) a management or governance plan; and (d) a financial plan (Hill, 1996).

Arizona is considered to have the least restrictive charter laws in the nation, in which charter schools are exempt from all state statutes and rules relating to schools. The state has taken a hands-off approach to monitoring charter schools and has lowered the reporting requirements for financial record keeping (Garn, 1998).

Considerable autonomy and independence is also given to Texas charter schools. Under Texas law, three types of charters are allowed: Home-Rule Education Districts; Campus or Program Charters; and Open-Enrollment charters. A Home-Rule District Charter, which must be authorized by local district voters, frees the district from most state requirements, including curriculum, employment, exit-level testing, and student discipline (Texas Education Code §12.001–12.030). The Campus Program charter, granted by a local district board of trustees, allows a campus or special program within a campus to operate free of most state and district requirements including district instructional and academic provisions (TEC §12.051–12.064).

The third type of charter option in Texas is the Open-Enrollment charter (TEC §12.101-12.118). Open-enrollment charter schools are far more popular than the other two charter options, which may be attributable to the application process that by-passes local school boards and allows organizers to go directly to the State Board of Education, thus creating new independent school districts that may cross existing district lines, and funding that follows the student (Patrick, 1999).

Admission policies of charters granted under this provision are prohibited from discrimination on the basis of sex, national origin, ethnicity, religion, disability, or academic or athletic ability, but a student with a history of discipline problems may be excluded. Open-enrollment charter schools in Texas receive 100% of state and district operations and maintenance funds from the state, according to their Weighted Average Daily Attendance (WADA). Charter schools may not charge additional tuition, although grants and fund-raisers are allowed.

A few charter school districts are beginning to surface. According to Patrick (1997), the entire Kingsburg Joint Union Elementary School District in California was one of the first to establish a charter school district, freeing the 1,800-pupil district from rigid state requirements and policies intended for larger districts. In July, 2000, Florida Governor Jeb Bush and the Florida Cabinet approved a plan that made Volusia County the first charter school district in the state. Volusia County has over 60,000 students and 65 schools. In exchange for a promise that student performance will improve, the entire school district is to be free from state regulations. Volusia Superintendent William Hall believes that creating charter districts will significantly improve student achievement more than any other school reform. The school district outlined 29 performance goals to boost achievement, including an increase each year in graduation rates, a decrease in student absenteeism, and increased family and community involvement (Rado, 2000).

State Legislation

Charter school laws in each state differ in the kinds and number of charter schools in the state, as well as in the level of freedom and amount of accountability that the charter schools will have. Significant criteria have been identified to determine the strength of the state statutes, that is, the degree to which the charter schools are likely to challenge the status quo educational system. These include: (a) who grants the charter; (b) who sponsors the charter; (c) how the charter can be formed; (d) exemptions from laws, rules, and policies; (e) fiscal autonomy; (f) legal autonomy; (g) maximum number and variety of charters; and (h) personnel qualifications. All of these components center around two essential qualities for charter school viability: autonomy and choice (Bierlein & Mulholland, 1994; Bierlein, 1995, Buechler, 1996).

In 14 states the local board is the only granting authority, and in 8 of those states, the local board decision can be appealed. In other states, charter granting agencies include State Boards of Education, local school boards, and universities. Each of the 37 charter laws allow public schools to convert to charter status, and all but Mississippi allows start-up schools to be created as charter schools. Charter schools are established as limited-term contracts, which means that at the end of a specified contract period, usually 3 to 5 years, the charter must be renewed. Although Arizona and the District of Columbia have 15-year contract terms, they do require review at the end of 5 years (*The State of Charter Schools 2000*, 2000).

Financing Charter Schools

Charter schools receive the tax monies that would normally go to the attending students' home schools. Charter sponsors usually supplement revenue with funds from private sources. Additionally, charter school sponsors must find and fund their own buildings (Unger, 1999). One of the early issues concerning charter schools has been the difficulty of starting a school without the support of a public school district. Locating and maintaining a building and purchasing curriculum is not only difficult but expensive. Some charter schools have supplemental funding from for-profit educational management organizations (EMOs) such as Tesseract or Edison. These EMOs have provided some charter schools with administrative support in the start-up years (Plank, Arsen, & Sykes, 2000). For additional information on EMOs, see chapter five.)

Accountability

All charters, in some way, are held accountable for student outcomes, but educators have yet to agree on accountability plans for charter schools. The District of Columbia Public Charter School Board believes that an on-site visit guided by a school's "self-study" is the best way to evaluate a new charter school. The local school board of education also approves charters but evaluates by way of a review team that is guided by a compliance checklist instead of self-study.

Even though charter schools are held accountable in very diverse ways based on the state and/or district, they have much more autonomy than traditional neighborhood schools. Because state regulatory practices differ greatly across the United States, there are varying amounts of monitoring. According to *The State of Charter Schools 2000* (2000), a fourth-year report, monitoring occurred most frequently in school finances (94%), compliance with legislative mandates (88%), student achievement (87%), and student attendance (81%). Other areas that were frequently monitored were student instructional practices, school governance, student completion, and student behavior. Nearly all charter schools have procedures in place, or are adopting procedures, to report on the school's progress to their governing boards, parents, community, funding sources, the chartering agency, and the State Department of Education.

Most charter schools (96%) use standardized test results for accountability purposes. However, other assessment methods are being incorporated, such as performance assessments, parent satisfaction surveys, and student surveys. Some schools also incorporate student portfolios into their student assessment policies.

As described earlier, charter schools that fail to live up to the terms of their contracts or lose significant numbers of students will be forced to close. As of December 2000, failed charter schools totaled 86 (4%) of the overall number opened, and these closures have attracted a great deal of media attention. As a result, some have questioned the validity of charter schools as a viable school reform, but Allen (2001) argues, "The question for observers and policy makers shouldn't be whether or not charter schools fail, but whether or not all schools, regardless of their category, are so sufficiently accountable that their lack of progress would lead to their closure."

Advantages and Disadvantages of Charter Schools

Advantages of charter schools have been identified as: (a) the ability of the consumer, or parent, to choose a public school setting that better serves their particular family; (b) increased consumer satisfaction in making a deliberate choice for their child's school; (c) increased parent participation; (d) devel-

opment of innovative educational practices; (e) higher income-earning opportunities for outstanding teachers with particular expertise; and (f) academic and psychological benefits for students (Finn, Manno, & Bierlein,
1996; Patrick, 1999; Taebel et al., 1997, Taebel et al., 1998).

Potential disadvantages that have surfaced include concerns about (a) re-
segregation of schools; (b) unscrupulous business or academic practices that
may go undetected for a period of time; (c) inconsistent curriculum throughout the United States; (d) underutilization of existing public school buildings;
and (e) taxpayer abandonment of a commitment to traditional public schools
(Finn, Bierlein, & Manno, 1996; Patrick, 1999; Taebel et al., 1997; Taebel et
al., 1998).

Teacher, Parent, Student Satisfaction

Generally, research findings about charter schools indicate a high level of
teacher satisfaction regarding their curriculum, teaching, and class size (Finn,
Manno, & Bierlein, 1996; Harris, Lowery, & Carr, 2000). Compared with
teachers in a traditional public school, these teachers feel a sense of empow-
erment in the classroom and are satisfied with their autonomy, influence,
freedom, and flexibility in classroom matters (Bomotti, Ginsberg, & Cobb,
1999). A teacher in a Texas charter school explained, "Because we're small,
we communicate with each other as teachers about what is happening in our
kids' lives at home, as well as in school" (Harris, in press). Another charter
school in Texas was started specifically to serve children with learning disabilities. The principal of this school commented, "Many children come to us
so defeated . . . but we are committed to do whatever we can to help a child
experience success" (in press).

Parents and children who choose charter schools also indicate a high level
of satisfaction with their charter schools (Taebel et al., 1997). A mother of a
Texas charter school fourth grader said that her son used to hate school, but
"now he actually likes getting up and going to school." A ninth-grade student
said that he loves his charter school because "they don't have cliques, race, or
anything here, we're all friends" (Harris, in press). One of the advantages for
parents choosing a charter school is that they can take their child out of the
school if the child is not successful.

A need for improved communication and involvement seemed to motivate
some parents to select charters schools. One parent who shared this belief

commented, "Communication with parents of secondary students is *inadequate!* We want to be involved in our children's lives!" (Patrick, 1999).

Another parent of a ninth grader in Texas explained their consideration of a charter school as a function of the state's accountability system: "I believe that as long as the current system is in place that grades our schools, more and more students will be moving to the charter schools." Other reasons cited by parents included class size, student-to-teacher ratio, and violence in the public schools and other safety issues. A comment from a sixth grader's parent demonstrated the competitive factor as it related to the size of many public schools: "Charter schools provide a choice and competition for large public schools" (Patrick, 1999).

Summary

Charter schools experienced rapid growth in the United States during the 10-year period of 1992 through 2002. Whether the charter school expansion will be sustained is yet to be seen. In reality, however, the greater impact of charter schools may lie with the school community at large, as traditional public schools began to react to greater market saturation. As stated by Patrick (1997), "Clearly, charter schools and school choice are envisioned as having the capacity to disrupt the status quo in educational bureaucracy." The question then becomes not will charter schools corner a larger percentage of the educational marketplace, but will their existence encourage widespread improvements in public education?

Internet Resources

- *http://www.ed.gov/pubs/charter4thyear/ack.html*
- *http://www.edreform.com/charter*
  Center for Education Reform
- *http://www.cde.ca.gov/ftbranch/retdiv/charter/index.html*
  California Department of Education
- *http://www.state.ct.us/sde/charter.htm*
  Charter School Information

- *http://www.policy.com/issuewk*
  Speak Out.Com–Policy News and Information Service
- *http://www.topschools.com*

Chapter References

Allen, J. (2001, January). Charter schools today: Changing the face of American education. Center for Education Reform. [Online]. Available: *http://www.edreform .com/pubs/cs_closures.htm.*

Bierlein, L. A. (1995, September). Charter schools: A new approach to public education. *NASSP Bulletin*, 79 (572), 12–20.

Bierlein, L. A., & Mulholland, L. A. (1994, September). The promise of charter schools. *Educational Leadership*, 52, 34-35, 37–40.

Bomotti, S., Ginsberg, R., & Cobb, B. (1999). Teachers in charter schools and traditional schools: A comparative study. *Education Policy Analysis*, 7 (22). [Online]. Available: *http://epaa.asu.edu/epaa/v7n22.html.*

Buechler, M. (1996, January). *Charter schools: Legislation and results after four years.* Bloomington, IN: Indiana Education Policy Center.

Budde, R. (1988). *Education by charter: Restructuring school districts.* Andover, MA: Regional Laboratory for Educational Improvement of the Northeast and Islands.

CER National Charter School Directory 2000. (2000). The Center for Education Reform. [Online]. Available: *http://www.edreform.com/press /nscd2000.htm.*

Charter Schools in California (2000). The Center for Education Reform. [Online]. Available: *http//edreform.com/charter_schools/states/california.htm.*

Charter School Legislation: State Rankings (2000). The Center for Education Reform. [Online]. Available: *http://www.edreform.com/charter_schools/laws/ranking. _2000.htm*

Chubb, J. E., & Moe, T. M. (1990). *Politics, Markets, and America's Schools.* Washington, DC: Brookings Institution.

Finn, C. E., B. V. Manno, & L. A. Bierlein. (1996). *Charter schools in action: What have we learned? First-year report.* Washington, DC: Hudson Institute.

Garn, G. (1998). The thinking behind Arizona's charter school movement. *Educational Leadership*, 56 (2), 48–50.

Harris, S. (In press). Children with special needs and school choice: 5 stories. *Preventing School Failure.*

Harris, S., Lowery, S., & Carr, C. (2000, November). *A comparative study of teacher attitudes of job satisfaction in public and private schools of choice.* Paper presented at the annual meeting of University Council of Educational Administration, Albuquerque, NM.

Hill, P. (1996, June). The educational consequences of choice. *Phi Delta Kappan*, 77, 671–675.

Overview of Charter Schools USCS. [Online]. Available: *http://www.uscharterschools.org/lpt/uscs_docs/58.*

Patrick, D. (1997, Fall/Winter). The role of charter schools in the reinvention of public education. *Teacher Education and Practice*, 13, 1–14.

Patrick, D. P. (1999). The response of a public school district to charter school competition: An examination of free-market effects. (Doctoral dissertation, University of North Texas, 1999. [Online]. Available: *http://www.unt.edu.*

Plank, D., Arsen, D., & Sykes, G. (2000). Charter schools and private profits. *The School Administrator*, 57 (4), 12–18.

Rado, D. (2000, July 12). Florida approves charter district. *St. Petersburg Times On-Line.* [Online]. Available: *http://sptimes.com/News/071200/news_pf/State/Florida_approves_char.shtml.*

Taebel, D., Barrett, E. J., Brenner, C.T., Kemerer, F., Ausbrooks, C., Clark, C., Thomas, K., Briggs, K. L., Parker, A., Weiher, G., Matland, R., Tedin, K., Cookson, C., & Nielsen, L. (1997, December). *Texas open-enrollment charter schools: Year one evaluation.* A research report presented to the Texas State Board of Education.

Taebel, D., Barrett, E. J., Chaisson, S., Kemerer, F., Ausbrooks, C., Thomas, K., Clark, C., Briggs, K. L., Parker, A., Weiher, G., Branham, D., Nielsen, L., & Tedin, K. (1998, December). *Texas open-enrollment charter schools: Year two evaluation.* A research report presented to the Texas State Board of Education.

Texas Education Code. (1998). *Texas school law bulletin.* Austin: West Publishing.

Unger, (1999). *School Choice: How to select the best schools for your children.* New York: Checkmark Books.

U.S. Department of Education. The state of charter schools 2000—fourth-year report. (2000). Washington, DC: Author.

Vanourek, G., Manno, B. V., Finn, C. E., & Bierlein, L. A. (1997, July). *Charter schools in action: The Educational Impact of Charter Schools.* Washington, DC: Hudson Institute.

Chapter Four

Public Alternative Schools

Michael H. Hopson, Ph.D.

Introduction

Webster's *New World Dictionary* defines the adjective "alternative" to mean: providing or being a choice between two, or less strictly more than two, things. By definition, then, an alternative school is a school that is a choice between at least two schools. The defining characteristic of an alternative school is, therefore, that which differentiates it from the other choice. Private schools, parochial schools, magnet schools, charter schools, and homeschools are all examples of alternatives to public schools. For the purposes of this chapter, public alternative schools will be considered to be academic alternative schools that are organized around a specific curriculum delivery.

Early in educational history, religion based schools provided the most common alternative to public education. Perhaps as a by-product of societal upheaval in the late 1960s and early 1970s, alternative schools began to appear, offering idealistic havens for students "turned off" by the traditional public school organization, discipline, and curricula. Many of these schools incorporated the phrases "free school" or "open school" in their names to indicate a progressive education philosophy (McGee, 2001). The recent increase in the number of alternative schools can be attributed to concerns about student safety and the resulting legislative mandates. In addition, research regarding how students learn has focused education reform on restructuring the traditional school environment.

The alternative schools that were created as a result of legislative mandates have, for the most part, been targeted at disruptive students who are assigned rather than permitted to choose the school they attend. These schools were initially organized on the premise that the student, not the system, is the problem (Gregory, 2001). The experiences of these schools in dealing successfully with the "problem students" caused educators to reexamine the factors influencing student performance. Even though these schools were created to serve a limited subset of the student population, they frequently served as the genesis for alternative programs designed to address the differing needs of students and parents.

Alternative schools have been created to assist communities in dealing with language barriers, as well as to promote cultural diversity. Many districts have chosen to address the economic problems related to population growth and an increasingly diverse population by creating "open enrollment" alternative schools. These schools allow the district to have increased flexibility in dealing with new facilities and attendance zones. In response to parental preference, some community schools have been organized around a specific educational philosophy. As public demands for accountability increase, alternative schools may become the public schools' answer to the economic threat posed by vouchers.

Structure

The public academic alternative schools that provide "school choice" for parents and students can be characterized according to curriculum, delivery system, and philosophy. Alternative schools today serve elementary, middle-school, and high school students. Generally, the alternative schools have been established in response to community needs and interests. These needs may be cultural, economic, and/or philosophical.

Elementary Schools

The Family School is an alternative program offered by the Albuquerque Public Schools. It combines multiage, open-ended curricula with home-based instruction in order to give parents a more active role in their children's education. Students attend four half-days a week and must participate in an additional 15 hours per week of home instruction. The home curriculum provides one-on-one instruction that can be used for enrichment, remediation, or independent study. The school is accredited by the State of New Mexico and participates in the district's annual review. The district operates the school under a Collaborative School Improvement Waiver, granted by the Department of Education (Albuquerque Public Schools, 2001).

In Ohio, the Douglas Alternative Elementary School operates as an open-space, whole language, arts-impact school. The building, designed with free-flowing flexible classrooms clustered around a central library, is located within walking distance of downtown Columbus. The school is supported by a community association comprised of parents, community members, and other friends of Douglas. Parents and other volunteers assist with reading computers, class projects, and field trips. The integrated curriculum focuses on the rich diversity in the city. Teachers use thematic units, the arts, and multiple learning strategies to help students progress at their own rate (Douglas Alternative School, 2001).

Five elementary alternative schools are operated by the Arlington Public Schools in Virginia. Each is organized around a different concept, but all are rated by the state using the Virginia School Performance Report Card. Two of the schools are characterized by the instructional methodology used, while the other three feature a foreign language immersion program. As the name implies, Arlington Traditional School uses traditional instruction with no team teaching or grouping of students. Admission is by application and lottery. Drew Elementary also serves kindergarten through fifth grade, but uses a more modern approach to instruction, featuring multi-age grouping and team teaching. Abingdon, Key, and Oakridge Elementary Schools offer Spanish immersion programs. English- and Spanish-speaking students in these programs are grouped together to receive math and science instruction in Spanish, and language arts and social studies in English (Arlington Public Schools, 2001).

Fairfax County Public Schools in Virginia offer two schools, Bailey's Elementary School for the Arts and Sciences and Hunters Woods Elementary School for the Arts and Sciences, as alternatives to traditional education. Bailey's Elementary integrates the arts and technology with instruction to make learning a creative experience. Students conduct research, produce live dramatic performances, compose original music scores, design science experiments, and build museum exhibits. Using the conceptual unit approach to instruction, students make connections across subject areas. At Hunters Woods, the goal is to establish a collaborative family of learners to focus innovations in teaching and learning. In partnership with George Mason Institute of the Arts, the school focuses on developing the student's powers of observation and creativity through music, theater, and dance (Fairfax County Public Schools, 2001).

The school board in Fort Collins, Colorado, created three alternative schools in order to "provide a level of educational choice that meets the increasingly diverse expectations of the community." The Core Knowledge

School stresses character education and discipline using the Cultural Literacy curriculum developed by E. D. Hirsch. The Lab School offers a nontraditional school setting that emphasizes a small pupil-teacher ratio and a child-centered, developmental curriculum. The Harris Bilingual Immersion School, as the name implies, features a strong bilingual language and cross-cultural program for Spanish- and English-speaking students (Bomotti, 1996).

Middle Schools

The middle-school students in Arlington may continue their Spanish immersion program in Kenmore Middle School. Kenmore uses the arts and communications technology to teach the district's middle-school curriculum. The integrated curriculum is based on Howard Gardner's work with Multiple Intelligences. In addition, the arts curriculum features an Artist in Residence Series that provides the opportunity for professionals to spend time sharing their expertise with the students (Arlington Public Schools, 2001).

The Alternative Community School of Ithaca, New York, is a small middle–high school for grades 6 through 12. The approximately 260 students are selected by random from an applicant pool. The school's philosophy is based on the premise that students have the right to make decisions about their own education. The curriculum is designed to give students the opportunity to study subjects of particular interest. Written evaluations are used as part of a Graduation by Exhibition system. In addition, the school strives to model a meaningful and respectful community. Students and teachers are involved in the governance of the school. Twice-weekly committee meetings are used as the vehicle for participatory management. Family groups and a combination of homeroom, support groups, and counseling are an integral part of the school. These groups of 8 to 14 students further establish the sense of a learning community (Ithaca Community School District, 2001).

High Schools

Most secondary alternative schools are organized to provide the core requirements for a high school diploma through flexible delivery systems. The most common systems include independent study, flexible scheduling, accelerated learning, and computer-assisted instruction. Other alternatives may be focused on career preparation, school-to-work programs, and advanced classes. The popularity of the Internet has generated a proliferation of virtual high schools.

The San Jose, California, Unified School District's Broadway High School has an objective of providing an alternative high school setting for students who achieve a greater measure of success in a small and more personalized educational environment. The school uses non-traditional methods to encourage success. The school offers vocational skills and job placement through a cooperative arrangement with a local occupational center. Other students access advanced placement courses through the local community college (San Jose Unified School District, 2001).

Individualized learning, small-group instruction, and personally designed curricular projects characterize the program at Clear View High School in Ferndale, Washington. Students are required to meet normal high school requirements, but the curriculum is delivered in a flexible and challenging structure. Individualized projects, field trips, one-to-one tutoring, computer-aided learning, and guest speakers are all used to tailor instruction for individual needs. The target population for the alternative program is that of students who: (1) choose to be educated in a nontraditional setting; (2) are employed part-time off-campus; and (3) are not benefiting from a traditional setting (Ferndale School District, 2001).

The secondary alternative school in Arlington, Virginia, H-B Woodlawn Secondary Program, is designed for students who can benefit from having more control over their education. The focus is on students who need less restriction and more freedom to be successful in schools. The faculty focuses the students on self-motivation and self-discipline. In addition, H-B Woodlawn places a greater emphasis on independent study and student-proposed nine-week elective courses. These courses have included philosophy, Japanese, Camping on Civil War battlefields, scriptwriting, popular culture, and independent film study. Another unique component of the program is that students retain their membership in their homeschool, and thus retain the option to participate in extracurricular activities, achieve class rank, and receive their diploma. Students are required to apply and are accepted through a lottery system (Arlington Public Schools, 2001).

Bryant Alternative High School in Fairfax County, Virginia, is one of several public campuses that offer non-traditional settings for students. The school features open enrollment, extended day classes, summer evening classes, and accelerated instruction. Other secondary schools in the Fairfax district are alternative in the sense that the curricula at each is focused on specific career interests. These high school academies offer advanced technical and specialized elective courses related to the career focus of the academy.

Secondary alternatives are also provided in the form of the International Baccalaureate Program at six district secondary schools (Fairfax County Public Schools, 2001).

Finances

All public alternative schools are financed by the local district. Funds may be generated in the same manner as for other public schools, using student enrollment and/or attendance data. In special situations, "start-up" allowances may be provided for the first few years of operation. In the schools that are organized around specific subject areas, additional funds may be allocated to enhance instruction (i.e., field trips, guest speakers, additional technology). Some supplement the budget using fund-raising through parent and community organizations. Many are supported through grants and partnerships with local businesses. "Over the years, many educators have concluded that the only way to ensure the creation and long-term success of an alternative is to use regular district funding formulas" (Barr & Parrett, 1997, p. 181).

Accountability

All public alternative schools are accountable to the state educational departments. In states that have mandatory testing, alternative schools are generally required to administer the same tests in which traditional neighborhood public schools participate. The schools may be given temporary exemptions for the first year or more. In some states, the accountability system or report card is applied in exactly the same manner for alternative schools as for regular campuses. In other states, the system has minor modifications that address the special circumstances inherent in alternative schools. Often, the alternative school receives a waiver for the initial years of existence.

Advantages and Disadvantages

Alternative schools provide a vehicle for parents to take a more active role in their child's education. In addition, alternative schools allow both the student and teacher to be more flexible in addressing student needs. In some districts, alternative schools may address language and cultural issues. Especially, at the secondary level, students who have an interest in or a need to graduate early are frequently able to do so because of the nature of the curriculum structure.

Unfortunately, alternative schools have the potential for increasing the separation of students by race, social class, and cultural background. In addition, parents choosing alternative schools tend to be those who are already active participants in their children's education. Sometimes, this level of parental involvement has the potential to become intrusive; additionally, some parents are not willing to welcome students who do not fit the mold (Bomotti, 1996). Therefore, too often a significant segment of the population at which alternative schools are targeted does not take advantage of the program.

Summary

As American society has evolved, the issues facing the public schools have changed drastically. Alternative schools are a response to the changing needs of public school students. Because the increasing emphasis on accountability has added impetus to the school reform movement, public school districts have identified alternative schools and programs not only as a means of improving student performance but also as a response to the call for vouchers and school privatization.

The alternative schools vary in curricula, teaching strategies, discipline management systems, and governance structures. Whatever the organizational structure, the goals are essentially the same: to address the individual needs of the students, to encourage more active parental involvement, and to maximize student success.

Additional Resources

- *http://www.educationrevolution.org*
- *http://www.ncacs.org*
- *http://www.alternativeschoolsnetwork.com*
- *http://www.mpls.k12.mn.us/schools/school_guide/alternative_school.shtml*
- *http://www.fcps.k12.va.us/about/specpro.htm*

- *http://www.arlington.k12.va.us/schools*
- *http://www.ferndale.wednet.edu/alths*
- *http://www.sjusd.k12.ca.us/sites/high/Broadway/about.html*
- *http://www.mpls.k12.mn.us/schools/school_guide/alternative_school.shtml*

Chapter References

Albuquerque Public Schools. (2001). Alternative Programs. [Online]. Available: *http://www.aps.edu/aps/district.altprograms.htm.*

Arlington Public Schools. (2001). Alternative Programs. [Online]. Available: *http://www.arlington.k12.va.us/schools.*

Barr, R. & Parrett, W. (1997). *How to create alternative, magnet, and charter schools that work.* Bloomington, IND: National Educational Service.

Bomotti, S. (1996).Why do parents choose alternative schools? *Educational Leadership,* 54 (2), 30.

Conrath, J. (2001). Changing the odds for young people. *Phi Delta Kappan,* 82 (8), 585–587.

Douglas Alternative School. (2001). *School Policy Manual.* Columbus, Ohio.

Fairfax County Public Schools. (2001). High Schools. [Online]. Available: *http://www.fcps.k12.va.us/schools.*

Ferndale School District. (2001). Alternative High School. [Online]. Available: *http://www.ferndale.wednet.edu/alths/.*

Gregory, T. (2001). Fear of success? Ten ways alternative schools pull their punches. *Phi Delta Kappan,* 82 (8), 577–581.

Ithaca Community Schools. (2001). [Online]. Available: *http://www.icsd.k12.ny .us/acs/.*

McGee, J. (2001). Reflections of an alternative school administrator. *Phi Delta Kappan,* 82 (8), 588–591.

San Jose Unified School District. (2001). Broadway High School. [Online]. Available: *http://www.sjusd.k12.ca.us/sites/high/Broadway/about.html.*

Chapter Five

Public Schools and Private Profit: The Challenge of Educational Management Organizations

Carolyn Carr, Ph.D.

Introduction

As the school reform movement of the 1990s swept the United States, the business community began to take increased notice as it perceived opportunities to step into the educational realm with the promise of producing quality education with a profit by employing proven business disciplines of efficiency and effectiveness. Privatization, actions that result in the transferal of students and resources from public schools to private schools or selected public schools, became the vehicle for this entrepreneurial movement. Many educators also saw a move toward privatization of schools as a potential remedy to the many administrative and instructional problems of public schools in a diverse society. The provision of quality alternative educational settings, school choice, appealed to many parents as well.

In response to these public concerns over cost and quality, Educational Management Organizations (EMOs) and the venture capitalists behind them have found a home in public schools through the legislatively established charter school movement. EMOs, "for-profit" private companies that provide school management and instructional services, are stepping in to manage many schools under public authority. EMO-managed public and private schools, unlike traditional public schools, are exempt under their contracts from many state and local school district policies. Public policy toward education has been to steer a course that embraces the public interest while allowing as much of the private interest as can be accommodated without bringing the two into serious conflict. This is a difficult charge that always places schools under a tension that is not easily resolved (Levin, 2001).

Involvement of private for-profit companies in the public school arena has both supporters and opponents. Information about the EMOs is available from both sources through their Web sites and publications, but should be viewed with an eye for the disparate viewpoints represented. Supporters of the privatization movement include such well-known organizations as the Cato Institute, the Center for Education Reform (CER), the Education Freedom Foundation, the Children's Educational Opportunity Foundation, Endives, the World Bank, the Heritage Foundation, and the National Center for Policy Analysis. Opponents are represented by equally prominent groups such as the National PTA, American Federation of Teachers (AFT), Anti-Defamation League (ADL), the National Education Association (NEA), People for the American Way, and Partners for Public Education. A more balanced perspective is presented by such groups as the Brookings Institution, the Education Commission of the States, Mathematica Policy Research, Inc., and Public Agenda (the National Center for the Study of Privatization in Education).

Legislation and Governance

Education has become a $740 billion market, 10% of which is comprised of private education companies, called variously EMOs, Educational Service Providers, and "edupreneurs" (Lips, 2001). Traditionally school districts have contracted with these enterprising companies for supplies, textbooks, food services, transportation, categorical programs, and other such distinct elements of managing schools. The first charter school opened in Minnesota in 1991, and since that time 37 states have passed laws to allow K–12 charter schools, thus opening the door for EMOs to provide extensive school services through charter schools or designated schools in public school districts, often including total management and instruction.

The authority to regulate traditional private schools has been left largely to the states by the U.S. Supreme Court, and these regulations have been modest in impact. The growing educational privatization movement in sub-contracting, charter schools, homeschools, and publicly funded voucher programs have been encouraged by this circumstance. Those who oppose this educational entrepreneurship or "edupreneurship" have sought limitations by imposing upon them similarly stringent accountability measures as those applied to public schools. These accountability measures appear in state constitutions, statutes, administrative agency regulations, charters, and contracts.

The challenge for state policy makers is to balance accountability with institutional autonomy (Kemerer, 2000).

The Center for Education Reform (CER) has developed a list of 10 factors by which it has ranked state policies on the levels of support or restriction of the development of autonomous charter schools. CER defines "strong laws" as those that *support* development, and "weak laws" as those that *inhibit* such development. These criteria are:

- *Number of schools:* Weak laws discourage growth by placing more constraints on the number of charter schools.

- *Multiple chartering authorities:* Weak laws discourage charter schools by bottlenecking the approval authority through a single entity—usually the local school board—and by providing a limited appeals process.

- *Eligible charter applicants:* Strong laws encourage growth by permitting a variety of individuals and groups both inside and outside the existing public school system to start charter schools.

- *New starts allowed:* Strong laws allow new schools to start up rather than permitting only public school conversions.

- *Formal evidence of local support:* Strong laws permit charter schools to be formed without proof of local support.

- *Automatic waiver from state and district laws:* Weak laws require charter schools to negotiate waivers on an issue-by-issue basis with charter-granting authorities rather than granting a blanket waiver. (Civil rights laws and health/safety codes are never waived.)

- *Legal/operational autonomy:* Strong laws permit charter schools to be independent legal entities instead of remaining under school district jurisdiction.

- *Guaranteed full funding:* Weak laws discourage growth by setting funding at less than 100% of the district's per-pupil or requiring negotiation.

- *Fiscal autonomy:* Strong laws give charter schools full control over their own budgets and funds.

- *Exemption from collective bargaining agreements/district work rules:* Weak laws do not give charter schools control over personnel decisions but make them subject to district collective bargaining agreements or work rules (*http://www.heartland.org/education/mar99/rankings.htm*).

Arizona, California, and Michigan (law passed in 1993) were among the earliest states to pass laws and are listed based on CER criteria among the 25 states with "strong laws." Eleven states are listed with "weak laws," and 14 had no laws at the time of the survey in 1999, though several states were considering such laws, and some states, including Oregon, have passed laws since that time. Not surprisingly the states with strongest laws have the vast majority of the charter schools (*http://www.heartland.org/education/mar99/rankings*). Of these charter schools, roughly 10 percent are run by for-profit companies (Lips, 2001). Arizona and Michigan, states with laws highly supportive of charter schools, have the lead in the numbers of EMO managed schools.

Financial Support

EMOs contracted by public schools to manage individual campuses within the school district often receive the same per-pupil allotments as do other schools in the same district. Special program funds such as those for special education and English language learners also frequently follow the students to the for-profit schools. In addition to these government funds, venture capital provides foundation support for the for-profit companies.

Education Week/KnowledgeQuest Ventures surveyed the growing interest of venture capital firms in the education industry in 1998. The results of that survey revealed key findings that clarify the rising interest in investing in the education industry in the near future.

> *The most important reasons for the venture capital firms' interest in the industry are a tie between potential return on investment (ROI) and the combined factor of market size and growth rate, with 75% of the firms listing one of these answers as the #1 factor. In contrast, the least reported reason for their interest in the industry is concern about the state of U.S. education, which was listed last by almost 70% of the respondents. This suggests that venture capitalists segregate their investment decisions from altruistic motivations. Therefore, it is important for education entrepreneurs to communicate in the "language of business" by emphasizing market need, product quality, and management ability—rather than merely educational quality—when they seek venture financing (EI Market Analysis, 1998, p. 4).*

Foundations such as those established by industrial-era families like the Fords, the Carnegies and the Rockefellers have been traditional benefactors of reform in public schools. Today, however, there are new names among the venture capitalists providing support for schools, especially the EMOs. Among them, according to a report in *U.S. News,* are the Fishers, founders of The Gap Inc, who have pledged millions in support of the Edison Schools in San Francisco. A. A. Taubman, a shopping-mall developer and chairman of Sotheby's, helped launch the Leona Group, which runs charter schools in Michigan and Arizona. J. C. Huizenga, a manufacturer and evangelical Christian, founded his own for-profit company, National Heritage Academies, which adopted a strong moral component in its curriculum. The Walton family of Wal-Mart fame are also supporting the privatization movement (*U.S. News,* April 27, 1998).

Financial accountability data, though hard to obtain since EMOs are not bound by the same disclosure laws as are public schools, generally reveal that EMOs have yet to generate expected profits. Efficiency gains and scale economies are obvious ways to reduce costs but are difficult to attain in education since many have negative effects on student learning (Plank, Arsen, & Sykes, 2000). Even the most well-known management companies, such as Edison and Advantage, are still relying on their investors and contracting agencies' funding to remain solvent. A prime example of beleaguered EMOs is The Tesseract Group, which has been plagued with debt and litigation, and was forced in 2000 to sell its Academy of Business College and several of its charter schools to stem its mounting financial losses. The company's stock was removed from the NASDAQ stock market when its assets dropped below the market's criteria (Walsh, 2001).

Accountability

The primary marketing cry for the privatization of schools has included the claim that these entrepreneurial schools will improve student achievement. At this point the reports from supporters and opponents are contradictory and inconclusive. Few reports other than general indicators are forthcoming from most of the EMOs. Many of the research studies have been sponsored by either proponents or opponents of the for-profit companies, making findings suspect. In an NEA-sponsored study of 10 of Edison's oldest schools, all operating for at least four years, Miron and Applegate at Western Michigan University found that "on criterion-referenced tests—those that measure whether or not students meet prescribed state standards—Edison students' gains or losses mirror those of students in comparison groups examined, which included students from surrounding public school districts" (Miron & Applegate, 2001). Miron acknowledged that on norm-referenced tests comparing students with other students, the schools did show improvement from year to year. This study was unique in that the researchers contracted with NEA that they be allowed to publish the findings, regardless of the results.

In a novel experiment in Pennsylvania, the state board of control that oversees the troubled Chester-Upland schools has contracted not with one for-profit company but with three, creating an arrangement of cooperation and competition among them. Edison Schools, Mosaica Education Inc., and Learn Now will cooperate on teacher contracts and transfer of student records. Competition will determine parental choice of which of the diverse programs their students will choose (Walsh, 2001).

Advantages and Disadvantages

The combination of public school and private profit has raised key issues for educators, policy makers, and parents alike. Traditional public school educators have pursued their careers under an ethic of public service rather than personal gain. The EI Market Analysis survey referred to previously in this chapter reveals the challenges EMOs face in marketing their services to public school districts while at the same time seeking venture financing by emphasizing market demand, product quality, and management expertise.

In a policy paper prepared for the Cato Institute, Lips (2001) describes her vision of a fully competitive education marketplace and how it would differ from the current system:

- Edupreneurs would likely open schools with a wide variety of curriculums, instructional methods, and philosophies of education in order to serve and satisfy a diverse customer base.

- Edupreneurs would invest in research on and development of new technologies to facilitate the education process.

- Higher education would become more accessible and affordable for people with lower incomes and those in the work force.

- A customer-driven education system would weed out substandard schools and products more rapidly that does the current system.

- Edupreneurs would provide education services designed to prepare students to participate effectively in the new economy. (p. 14–15)

These claims have merit, but at the same time serious questions have arisen related to schools being managed by EMOs. While "privately financed companies bring to public schools external funding, technology, innovative instructional designs, and unique managerial and staffing designs" (Furtwengler, 1998, p. 47), they also face significant obstacles, including large initial and ongoing overhead costs. These costs can include facilities' rental or purchase, tests and materials, teaching and staff salaries, and marketing to attract students. Teachers' unions oppose the schools because they generally offer lower salaries and fewer benefits than do public schools. Because the schools exist within a legal system, there is the ongoing political risk of changes in government funding, state or local regulations, and legislative support (Kemerer, 2001; Levin, 2000; Lips, 2001). These limitations have resulted in few, if any, reports of financial profit among the many educational companies at this stage in their development. Other evaluative questions and thoughts related to the role of the EMOs in public schools systems include these:

- Can EMOs produce student educational outcomes that are equivalent or superior to that of traditional public schools while generating profit rates sufficient to attract private investors?

- Can EMOs generate profits from increased efficiency and improved performance—and not at the expense of students who remain in traditional public schools?

- Even if privately managed schools satisfy both of these efficiency conditions, thoughtful people may disagree as to whether they advance or undermine other values that are important in the public school system. (Plank, Arsen, & Sykes, 2000, p. 13)

An examination of the management practices of several of the largest EMOs reveals common strategies for cost saving. Whether these cost saving measures are utilized depends upon the laws in each state. Labor costs are frequently cut by employment of noncertified, younger, and less experienced teachers. Few of the EMOs participate in state retirement systems. These practices contribute to higher turnover and expense to school districts. Class sizes are sometimes larger than in neighboring public schools. Support services such as transportation, school lunches, interscholastic athletics, and band and orchestra programs are often eliminated or provided by low-wage firms or parent volunteers. Standardization of administrative practices, development of a system-wide curriculum, and targeting elementary rather than the more expensive secondary schools are further cost saving measures seen among for-profit schools that take advantage of economies of scale (Furtwengler, 1998; Levin, 2001; Molnar, 1994; Plank, Arsen, & Sykes, 2000).

When for-profit schools are unregulated by their sponsoring agency they have much more flexibility in rewarding valued teachers. For example, many employ various versions of merit pay, such as rewarding subject specialization and other talents, as well as career ladders unavailable to teachers in public schools. Professional development is also an area of difference as shown by Edison Schools, which provides as much as three weeks of training a year, whereas typical public schools may provide only three to five days per year, with little follow-up or assessment. Since professional development is a key to school effectiveness, this is an important strength in marketing for EMOs.

This same flexibility varies among the EMOs when principal leadership and curriculum and instruction are considered. Principals generally have wide discretion in decision making, hiring, and teacher assessment. On the other hand, most EMOs have highly structured curricula and instructional methods among their sites, unlike the traditional public schools that must respond to a diverse community with diffuse interests. As an example,Aadvantage Schools are marketed by promotion of direct instruction following a strictly prescribed curriculum that is exactly the same in all Advantage Schools.

Socioeconomic implications are another issue of importance when examining schools run by the for-profit EMOs. Through the sponsoring public agency, these schools often receive the same funding allowances for special students as do public schools, yet for-profit schools often limit or eliminate services to high-cost students such as the disabled or English language learners. Unlike public schools, they are frequently able to selectively admit students under their contracts. In an article in *U.S. News,* Lyle Voskuil, director of special education for National Heritage Academies in Grand Rapids, Michigan, is reported as saying "that for financial reasons his school offers no more than three hours of special-ed services to a student a week and that they urge the parents of students who need more help not to attend the schools"(The

New Educational Bazaar, 1998). This raises ethical questions as well as questions regarding the ability of EMOs to lead the way to general improvements in public education. Levin (1999) poses the issue in this way:

> *A major public purpose of schooling is to provide a common educational experience with respect to curriculum, values, goals, language, and political socialization so that students from many different backgrounds will accept and support a common set of social, political, and economic institutions. The challenge is whether a marketplace of schools competing primarily on the basis of meeting the private goals of parents and students will coalesce around a common set of social, political, and economic principles in the absence of extensive regulations or powerful social incentives. (p. 16)*

New Directions for EMOs: A Focus on Adults

A number of EMOs are moving beyond the K–12 market to post secondary education in response to the growing demand for teachers. This movement is an important challenge to the world of higher education, traditionally the provider of educators to public schools. Sylvan Learning Systems, long known as a provider of tutoring services to K–12 students, has now launched a wide variety of teacher skills courses and programs leading to state licenses for classroom teachers. The company anticipates expansion of these programs into a number of states.

In addition, the for-profit University of Phoenix is expanding the number of states in which it is permitted to prepare teachers for licensure. In some states this licensure preparation extends to providing licensure programs for school administrators as well. The University of Phoenix has also achieved regional accreditation status. Susan Mitchel, the dean of the University of Phoenix's college of education, is quoted as saying, "Our sole mission is to offer programs to working adults, and we are good at providing a location and services, and time and days of classes, and parking and the other conveniences the students find important" (For profits tapping into teacher training, 2000). Other educators question this expansion, suggesting that these programs are less rigorous and thorough than the traditional university programs, and that they mimic some of the for-profit K–12 programs in that they are scripted and inflexible.

Resources for More Information

On the pages that follow are brief overviews of eight major nationwide EMOs selected for inclusion because they operate K–12 schools in more than one state and have been in operation for at least four years. Overview, mission, curriculum, and accountability measures for each of the companies are described. Contact information has been included for the EMOs. Each company should be considered in light of the information earlier provided in this chapter.

Advantage Schools, Inc.
60 Canal Street
Boston, MA 02114
617-523-2220 phone
888-292-2344 phone
617-523-2221 fax
http://www.advantage-schools.com

Overview
Advantage, founded in 1996 by Steven F. Wilson, opened its first two schools in September 1997. It claims to be the nation's largest charter school management company, operating in at least 15 schools in eight states. Most schools open as elementary schools, growing by a grade per year through grade 12, though none has attained all 12 grades as yet. These schools are conducted in a formal environment with rigorous academic standards, "zero-tolerance" discipline policies, and a uniform dress code. According to its own reports, most advantage schools serve low-income urban students. A professional development coordinator at each school provides training and coaching for teachers and instructional assistants. Advantage has a seven-hour school day and a 200-day instructional year.

Mission
The mission of Advantage Schools is to create a new generation of world-class urban public schools that will enable all children—regardless of socio-economic background or prior academic performance—to reach the heights of academic achievement.

Curriculum
Direct formalized instruction (Direct Instruction Strategies for Teaching Arithmetic and Reading: DISTAR) forms the core of the Advantage instruc-

tional model, including beginning language, reading, and arithmetic. Students proceed through the curriculum based on skill level rather than on the traditional annual promotion patterns. Teachers deliver highly structured, scripted lessons in science, history, geography, foreign language, literature, music, and the arts in the classical liberal arts tradition under the direction of a "lead teacher" at each grade level. Younger students follow a phonics-based reading course. The learning environment is built around a structured character and ethics curriculum called "The Code of Civility." High school students receive an International Baccalaureate curriculum or a vocational training program. Classes are characterized as having low student-to-teacher ratios.

Achievement Reports

The Advantage Web site claims remarkable gains in students' academic performance, conduct, and self-confidence. Specific achievement data are not presented on the Web site.

Beacon Educational Management, Inc.

112 Turnpike Road, Suite 107
Westborough, MA 01581
800-789-1258 phone
508-836-2604 fax
http://www.beaconedu.com

Overview

Beacon, founded in 1992 in Westborough, Massachusetts, changed its name from Alternative Public Schools, Inc., in 1997. The Chief Operating Officer is Michael B. Ronan. Beacon provides full-service management services to existing and newly created K–12 charter or district schools, including financial, human resources, technology, special education and administrative support. The company Web site lists 24 schools in five states, with services for nearly 7,500 students (*http://www.beaconedu.com*). The company claims to improve education in public schools, particularly in low-income districts and with low-achieving students. The company reputedly has been a pioneer among EMOs with such practices as gaining the right to hire and fire district staff and providing on request only partial services such as financial record keeping, teacher recruitment, or food service rather than total management services. Teacher salaries are based on student achievement. Beacon also emphasizes the importance of mentoring and parental involvement (*http://www.aft.org /privatization/profiles/beacon.html*).

Mission

"In collaboration with local school personnel, Beacon seeks to help all children develop the necessary skills, knowledge, and values to function as effective and productive citizens in the 21st Century. To achieve this mission, Beacon draws upon a national data base of standards, a high-caliber curriculum, advanced instructional strategies and cutting-edge technology" (*http://www.beaconedu.com*).

Curriculum

The in-house curriculum is called Beacon Lightpoints and is designed in an initial assessment upon entering a community. Consequently the curriculum varies among the many Beacon sites, but generally includes a core knowledge sequence (*http://www.aft.org/privatization/profiles/beacon.html*). Beacon's website describes its curriculum as "standards based . . . to meet national, state, and local reports," including "School Tools™ for teachers and students" and delivered in a "year round, extended and traditional school year" (*http:www.beaconedu.com*).

Achievement Reports

No information is available on the company Web site.

Edison Schools

[THE EDISON PROJECT, LTD.]
521 Fifth Avenue, 16th Floor
New York, NY 10175
212-309-1600 phone
212-309-1604 fax
http://www.edisonschools.com

Overview

Generally recognized as the nation's leading for-profit contract and charter school company, Edison claims to be open to all students. Edison was founded in 1992 by President and Chief Executive Officer Christopher Whittle, and opened its first schools in 1995. Its marketing materials promise improved student performance through a longer school day and school year, and provide all students above third grade with laptop computers. According to the website, every member of the Edison national system is electronically connected via "The Common," Edison's intranet message, conferencing, and information system, allowing interschool communication and use of electronic resources including a digital library of periodicals and links to the World Wide Web" (*http://www.Edisonschools.com/overview/ov03.html*).

Mission

"We believe that every child should be given exciting educational opportunities and that every child has a tremendous capacity for learning. And, we believe that great schools are places that nurture the creative spirit, prize the beautiful as much as the useful, and inculcate a love of learning." (*http://www. Edisonschools.com/overview/ov03.html*)

Curriculum

Schools utilize "Success for All," a comprehensive reading program developed by Robert Slavin in which students are grouped by skill level, and University of Chicago "Everyday Mathematics." Edison prefers to operate schools of 600 students or more in which 120 to 150 students are assigned to a "house," and stay with core house teachers through several years.

Achievement Reports

Edison claims student achievement is steadily rising, with students on average gaining more than 5 percentiles per year on nationally normed tests and 7 percentage points on criterion-reference tests. Since opening, 85% of Edison schools have posted positive achievement trends. Specific test data are not readily available on the Edison Web site.

The Leona Group LLC

4660 South Hagadorn Road, Suite 500
East Lansing, MI 48823-5353
517-333-9030 phone
517-333-4559 fax
http://www.leonagroup.com

Overview

The Leona Group LLC company, founded by William Coats in 1997, is one of the few EMOs claiming to be making a profit, and this after only three years. In 1998–99 it had 25 charter schools in Michigan and Arizona, and served approximately 4,000 students. The company favors clustering schools within a state. Leona charges a set, yearly management fee to charter school boards. At many locations school staffers are offered pay incentives for increasing enrollment. All of Leona's teachers are currently required to have state certification. At the time of this writing the Web site was under construction.

Mission

Leona encourages a "nurturing, caring and challenging environment where each student receives personalized attention, experiences constant evaluation and support, encounters more hands-on learning, receives positive reinforcement and encouragement, is taught to read, write and think critically, discovers the meaning of excellence and success, learns to meet high academic and social standards" (*http://www.leonagroup.com/mieminfo.html*).

Curriculum

"Leona does not utilize a system-wide curriculum. Instead, it tailors a curriculum to the students and the community. . . . All Leona schools utilize team-teaching methods and stress computer literacy. In addition, the company advertises small class sizes, with student-to-teacher ratio at each site ranging from 15:1 to 25:1" (*http://www.aft.org/privatization/profiles/leona.html*).

Achievement Reports

No data available on company Web site.

National Heritage Academies
989 Spaulding Avenue, S.E.
Grand Rapids, MI 49546
800-699-9235 phone
http://www.heritageacademies.com

Overview

The National Heritage Academies program, founded by J. C. Huizenga, and opened its first school in 1995. Its president and CEO is Peter Ruppert. The National Heritage Academies is advertised as being grounded in the principles of Effective Schools Research associated with quantifiably improved student learning (*http://www.heritageacademies.com*). The company generally opens K–5 schools, averaging 250 to 300 in enrollment and subsequently adds grades as students progress. At this writing there are no high schools in the system. To encourage active parental involvement, parents sign contracts when their children enroll (*http://www.heritageacademies.com/academies_program .htm*).

Mission

The company mission is "to challenge students to achieve their greatest potential and deliver on the promise of higher standards, academic excellence and sound moral guidance" (*http://www.heritageacademies.com/academies_program.htm*).

Curriculum

National Heritage advertises a teacher-directed back-to-basics approach utilizing the Hirsch Core Knowledge Sequence for approximately 50% of it curriculum. This includes a phonics-based reading program and math delivery through such programs as the Chicago Everyday Mathematics program or Saxon Math. There is a strong moral focus that incorporates "the four universal Greek Cardinal Virtues of responsibility, justice, prudence and fortitude" throughout the curriculum (*http://www.heritageacademies.com/academies_program.htm*).

Achievement Reports

The company Web site asserts that "test results over the past two years show that students have scored 35% above the national average on standardized tests measuring grade level growth" (*http://www.heritageacademies.com/academies_program.htm*). No further information identifying tests or data were presented.

Nobel Learning Communities, Inc.

Rose Tree Corporate Center 11

1400 N. Providence Road

Suite 3055

Media, PA 19063

610-891-8200 phone

610-891-8222 fax

http://www.nobeleducation.com

Overview

Nobel Learning Communities was founded by Chairman and Chief Executive Officer Jack Clegg. Under his management, the Rocking Horse Childcare Centers of America sold its less profitable centers, and in December 1993 changed its name to Nobel Educational Dynamics. In January 1998, Knowledge Universe, a company owned by Michael Milken and Lawrence Ellison, purchased a substantial stake in Nobel. In December of the same year, the name of the company was changed to Nobel Learning Communities to convey a clearer and more positive image. (Its Ticker Symbol changed from NEDI to NLCI.)

According to its Web site, Nobel Learning Communities' schools are the largest preschool through eighth grade private school system in the United States, operating approximately 140 private schools in 13 states, and currently pursuing plans for further nationwide expansion. According to its Web site, the company targets moderate to middle-income families, children of blue-collar or white-collar workers, multiracial and various family backgrounds with an extended 12-hour school day and year-round programs. Nobel is accredited by NIPSA (National Independent Private School Association). Nobel schools typically hold between 150 and 250 students and have an average class size of 17 (*http://www.nobeleducation.com*).

Mission

Nobel Learning Communities' business mission is: "To be the leader in the United States in providing affordable private education from preschool through eighth grade for the children of middle-income working families . . . while maximizing shareholders' value."

Nobel Learning Communities' internal mission is: "To serve children from infancy through the eighth grade as the distinction in preschool and private school education. Nobel is committed to the highest developmental and educational standards to best ensure the personal growth and future achievement of our children. Nobel is dedicated to providing a secure and caring environment in partnership with the communities we serve. Our mission is children and their future. Nobel's education staff knows that accomplishing their internal mission will guarantee the success of the business mission" (*www .nobeleducation.com*).

Curriculum

Nobel schools require no entrance examinations. Nobel refers to its curriculum as "expanding," giving recognition to creativity through art, music, and other enrichment programs. Sports, theme clubs, summer programs, and learning technologies are featured. The company also characterizes its programs as developmental, with encouragement of interaction with adults and peers in order to develop appropriate social and cooperative work skills. The program is aimed to "develop the whole child, educationally, emotionally, culturally and socially" (*http://www.nobeleducation.com*).

Achievement Reports

Nobel claims its students achieve one to three years beyond national norms on the Stanford Achievement Tests, though no supporting data are provided on the Web site.

SABIS Educational Systems
6585 Beach Road
Eden Prairie, MN 55344
612-941-3500 phone
612-941-4015 fax
http://www.sabis.net

Overview

"Intered," owned by the SABIS Foundation, owns SABIS Educational Systems, the branch of the company that manages charter schools. SABIS was founded in Lebanon in 1886, in a suburb of Beirut. In 1975 it started an expansion program outside Lebanon. Its director general is Ralph Bistany, and its president is Leila Saad. SABIS is a rapidly expanding international school management company with 21 member schools, 3 associate member schools, and approximately 20,000 students. Member schools operate in the United States, the United Kingdom, Germany, Lebanon, Jordan, Egypt, Saudi Arabia, Qatar, the United Arab Emirates, and Pakistan.

Mission

"The school will be recognized as a provider of top quality education to a highly diverse student body. It will prepare all students for success in college, equip them with the ability and desire for lifelong learning, and strengthen their civic, ethical, and moral values. The school will maintain high standards of efficiency and accountability throughout its operation" (*http://www .sabis.net*).

Students are admitted and placed in heterogeneously grouped classes on the basis of a battery of tests in English and mathematics. SABIS claims a comprehensive, dynamic, and rigorous curriculum continually updated by the SABIS Academic Development Department. School goals include college preparation, mastery of English, mathematics, and a second language. Other goals include upholding high standards of ethical, moral, and civic conduct and the encouragement of informed decisions on social issues. Extracurricular activities, school management, and community work are also encouraged through the Student Life Organization (SLO). SABIS has its own curriculum and writes many of its own textbooks. Teaching methods are prescribed and include a point system included in each course syllabus.

Achievement Reports

SABIS has its own computerized system of testing, The Academic Monitoring System (AMS), which monitors student learning and progress through administratively designed course syllabi by adjusting instructional rate, focus, or placement. The Web site also claims regular external testing, but no details are given. Achievement scores are not listed on the website.

Other major EMOs include:
Aramark Educational Resources, Inc.
573 Park Point Drive
Golden, Colorado 80401
303-526-3421 (800-777-4331) phone
http://www.aramark.com

Mosaica Education, Inc.
4040 Civic Center Dr., Suite 200
San Rafael, CA 94903
415-491-1305 phone
http://www.mosaicaeducation.com/html

Tesseract Group
7900 Xerxes Ave. South
Minneapolis, MN 55431
612-832-0092 phone
http://www.tesseractgroup.org

Other Resources

- Links to Mixed Perspectives. National Center for the Study of Privatization in Education, Teachers College, Columbia University. [Online[. Available: *http://www.tc.columbia.edu/ncspe/LinklistMTXT.*
- Links to Privatization Opponents. National Center for the Study of Privatization in Education, Teachers College, Columbia University. [Online]. Available: *http://www.tc.columbia.edu/ncspe/LinklistOTXT.*
- Links to privatization supporters. National Center for the Study of Privatization in Education, Teachers College, Columbia University [Online]. Available: *http://www.tc.columbia.edu/ncspe/SlinklistTXT.*

Chapter References

Advantage Schools [Online]. Available: *http:// www.advantage-schools.com.*

Beacon Educational Management, Inc. [Online]. Available: *http://www .beaconedu.com.*

Center for Educational Reform [Online]. Available: (*http://www.edreform.com /pubs/chglance.htm*).

Charter School Legislation: State rankings, [Online]. Available: (*http://www.heartland.org/education/mar99/rankings.htm*).

Chubb, J., & Moe, T. (1990). *Politics, markets, and America's schools.* Washington, DC: The Brookings Institution.

Edison Schools [Online]. Available: *http://www.edisonschools.com.*

EI Market Analysis: Venture capital survey examines interest in education businesses. (November 1998). *The Education Industry Report,* p. 4.

For-profits tapping into teacher training. (March 29, 2000). *Education Week on the Web* [Online]. Available: *http://www.edweek.org/ew/ewstrory.cfm?slug=29profit.h19.*

Furtwengler, C. (1998). Heads up! The EMOs are coming. *Educational Leadership, 56* (2), 44–47.

Kemerer, F. R. (August 2000). Legal issues involving educational privatization and accountability. Occasional Paper No. 6. National Center for the Study of Privatization in Education [Online]. Available: *http://www.tc.columbia.edu/ncspe/indexframe .htm*).

The Leona Group LLC [Online]. Available: *http://www.leonagroup.com.*

Levin, H. M. (February 2001). Thoughts on for-profit schools. Occasional Paper No. 14. National Center for the study of Privatization in Education. [Online]. Available: *http://www.tc.columbia.edu/ncspe/indexframe.htm*).

Levin, H. M. (1999). The public-private nexus in education. *American Behavioral Scientist, 43,* 1, 124–137. [Online]. Available: *http://www.tc.columbia.edu/ncspe/indexframe .htm.*

Lips, C. (January, 2001). The promise of for-profit primary education. *Consumer's Research Magazine.* January 2001, 84, 1, pp. 10–15.

Miron, G., & Applegate, B. (2001). An evaluation of student achievement in Edison Schools opened in 1995 and 1996. [Online]. Available: *http://www.wmich.edu/evalctr .html.*

Molnar, A. (September, 1994). Education for profit: A yellow brick road to nowhere. *Educational Leadership, 54,* 1. [Online]. Available: *http://www.ascd.org /readingroom/edlead/9409/molnar.html.*

The National Heritage Academies [Online]. Available: *http://www.heritageacademies .com.*

The new educational bazaar. (1998, April 27). *U.S. News.* [Online]. Available: *http:// www.usnews.com/usnews/issue/980427/27char.htm.*

Nobel Learning Communities Inc. [Online]. Available: *http://www.nobeleducation .com.*

Plank, D. N., Arsen, D, & Sykes, G. (May 2000). Charter schools and private profits. *The School Administrator, 57* (5), 12–18.

SABIS Educational Systems. [Online]. Available: *http://www.sabis.net.*

Turning schools right side up, Editorial. (1999, Nov. 16). *Wall Street Journal.*

Walsh, M. (2001, April 4). In Pa., District tries 3-way contest to fix schools. *Education Week, XX,* 29, p. 1, 12–14.

Section Three

Private Schools of Choice

Sandra Harris, Ph.D.

In the early history of the United States, much of the education of children occurred in nonpublic places, such as the church and the home. Only in the New England colonies in the 17th century was public money used to educate children . . . an education that commingled church and state interests (Hlebowitsh & Tellez, 1997). However, as the nation grew and became more diverse, this idea became unmanageable and resulted in a dual system of schools: state-sponsored common (public) schools, and private schools financed by tuition independent from the public system.

According to the Council of American Private Education (CAPE), of the 53 million school children in America today, over 5,927,000 students are enrolled in private schools, which represents 11% of all students in the United States. In fact, one in four of the nation's schools is a private school; 85% of private schools are parochial (this includes all religious schools), and 81% have fewer than 300 students. The average tuition in 1993–94 was $3,116 per year, and over 75% of the children who attend private school come from families with annual incomes of less than $75,000 (CAPE, 2000).

Educational alternatives offered to private school students are wide-ranging. Independent schools offer a diverse curriculum from arts-focused schools to preparatory schools. Parochial schools, themed around religion, represent many denominations, such as Lutheran, Episcopal, and Jewish, but the Roman Catholic is the largest. The Catholic parochial education system has offered an alternative to public schooling since the 19th century and has over 8,600 elementary and secondary schools (The Exodus, 1991) which represent nearly 50% of all parochial schools (What's New, 1999).

Christian schools constitute the fastest growing system of private schools and include schools affiliated with a conservative Christian association. In 1989 these schools accounted for 16.7% of private school students; in 1997, this number had risen to 20.8% (What's New, 1999). Many Christian schools are sponsored by nondenominational churches, but these schools are also sponsored by conservative denominations, such as Baptist.

Another trend within this category of private schooling is the rise of homeschools. Today, in America over a million children are schooled at home, usually by the mother.

While nearly 90% of the nation's students attend public schools, the number of private schools increased nearly 30% in the 1980s (The Exodus, 1991), an increase that is projected to continue over the next ten years. Certainly, many parents and educators who choose private schools do so because of dissatisfaction with the public schools; however, 35% of parents who enroll children in private schools in America's metropolitan areas are not dissatisfied with public schools. These individuals choose private schools out of a "desire for alternatives" for their children (What's New, 1999).

This desire of parents and families to have more alternatives for their children's education is widening the consideration of choice into the private arena, which, at this point, is unavailable to many families because of limited income. Thus, issues, such as vouchers and tuition tax credits, are at the forefront of the political-educational arena today. Private schools consistently have a high track record of academic achievement (What's New, 1999) and extend schooling options for those who can afford them.

References

Council for American Private Education [CAPE]. (2000, February 12). The Council for American Private Education web page. [Online]. Available: *http://www .capenet.org/.*

The Exodus. (1991, December 9). *U.S. News & World Report*, p. 66–68.

Hlebowitsh, P. & Tellez, K. (1997). *American education: Purpose and promise.* Belmont, CA: West/Wadsworth Publishing Company.

What's New? (1999). Council for American Private Education. [Online]. Available: *http://www.capenet.org/new.html.*

Chapter Six

The Independent School

John Gooden, Ed.D.
Donnya Stephens, Ed.D.
Betty Alford, Ph.D.

Introduction

Private schools, prep schools, coeducational day or country day schools, boarding schools, military schools, single-sex schools, international schools, and religious schools are just some of the names used to refer to the hundreds of independent schools. Most independent schools are nonsectarian and steeped in the history and tradition of American education, while others are religious independent schools founded by various religious denominations or groups.

Independent schools vary in size, type, philosophy, tradition, history, cost, location, resources, and organizational structure. What they have in common is that they are independently governed, self-supporting, define their own curriculum, determine the qualities they want in both teachers and students, and are small educational communities (Kane, 1992a). Additionally, independent schools must be accredited by an approved state or regional association, and hold not-for-profit 501(c)(3) status (National Association of Independent Schools, 2000). It is in the area of self-governance, however, that independent schools truly vary from parochial schools. The independent school board of trustees has the ultimate authority over the school's mission, philosophy, program, and resources, whereas parochial schools (i.e., Catholic schools Lutheran schools, Baptist schools, etc.) are different from independent schools because the ultimate control is held by their religious hierarchy and clergy. Conversely, religious independent schools are loosely tied to their religious denomination and operate through an independent board of trustees.

The United States has approximately 114,800 schools, and the National Association of Independent School (NAIS), an advocacy organization for independent schools, claims that currently over 1,025 of these schools are NAIS member schools. Of the member schools, 84% are coeducational schools, 9%

are girls' schools, and 7.4% are boys' schools. Of the total student population (472,967), 18% are minority students and international students comprise 2.4% (National Association of Independent Schools, 2000).

According to the Southern Association of Independent Schools, parents choose independent schools for reasons of preparation for college level study, cultural opportunities, safe environments, parent involvement, outstanding teachers, school organization, and social environments. Increasingly, after such events as the Columbine shooting, parents have turned to independent schools as a perceived safe haven for their child. In addition, as the competition for admission to the nation's top colleges and universities has intensified, parents are seeking independent schools to prepare students more fully for college admission. In the 1990s, public schools came under attack for lowered standards, violence, and uncertified teachers. Since independent schools have largely remained unscathed by these attacks, the enrollment in independent schools has been on the rise (Southern Association of Independent Schools, 2001). Parents are selecting independent schools in hopes of providing a higher quality education for their children than they perceive many public schools now afford to students.

For many years, independent schools were perceived as an enclave for white, wealthy families; however, increasingly concerned parents of diverse ethnic groups and socioeconomic populations now advocate school choice. For example, a recent television public service announcement airing in Washington, DC featured an African-American parent concerned about the quality of her particular neighborhood school stating, ". . . I didn't get a good education, and I'm stuck in a dead-end job. I want more for my daughter. That's why I'm for school choice." Increasingly, parents of diverse ethnic and socioeconomic backgrounds have sought to address their concerns about the quality of academic education available for their child in public schools by seeking independent schools as a legitimate option for their child.

Another reason that parents select independent schools relates to the emphasis on the whole child. According to Levison (1994), the mission and objectives of most independent schools promote educating the "whole child" in terms of cognitive and affective development. Also, independent schools embrace a strong student-teacher relationship, and the curriculum for these schools usually promotes self-discipline versus external discipline (Tauber, 1995). Moreover, independent schools generally are smaller and have a smaller teacher-pupil ratio than public schools. A smaller class size facilitates small group and one-on-one instruction for promoting greater skill attainment. Smaller class sizes also are more conducive to the development of relationships wherein each individual student participates in a caring relationship with an adult in the school versus the anonymity and estrangement that can often characterize the large, urban schools. In developing the whole child, the strong relationships between students and the adults at the schools that are fostered by the small school setting leads many parents to seek independent schools (1995).

Structure

Organization

It is the responsibility of the independent school board of trustees to hire the school's chief administrator. The school's administrator is an extremely powerful individual who, besides working closely with the trustees, has the ultimate responsibility for the operation of the school. The administrator is a highly visible advocate and spokesperson for the school's educational mission and goals, and is responsible for financial management, fund-raising, and plant and facilities management, as well as strategic planning.

The strength of a good administrator is the ability to develop a good administrative team. Although the organizational structure of independent schools varies, the administrator delegates authority to an administrative team that carries out the daily functions of the school. These individuals are usually known as assistant heads; upper, middle, or lower school division heads; deans; and directors. These organizational hierarchies are somewhat complex, and most administrators have some teaching responsibilities.

Teaching and Learning

The curriculum is the heart of a school, and teaching and learning is its lifeblood. The independent school's curriculum is what makes the school competitive. It is the curriculum that brings to life the mission, philosophy, values, and beliefs of the independent school. Independent schools are able to espouse a wider range of beliefs and values and to teach subjects that sometimes are not permitted in public schools.

Independent schools are required to meet their state curricular standards, yet, in an effort to achieve excellence and to be competitive, independent school curricula often exceed those standards required by states. For many schools, the independent secondary school curricula are college preparatory with arts and music programs. There is also a strong emphasis on character, moral, religious, and physical development in most schools. Additionally, independent schools have strong athletic and extracurricular programs, and many schools are noted for the service component of their programs (Kane, 1992; Unger, 1993).

Students

Admission to independent schools is determined by student supply and demand. Admission is a dual process in that while the school is deciding if the candidate has the potential to develop and grow within their community, the child and the family are deciding as well if the school is an appropriate learning and social environment for the student. Gaining admission to to a school usually involves completing an application, an interview, and a review of school transcripts. Also, secondary school students are also required to take one of the following standardized examinations: Secondary School Admission Test (SSAT) or Independent School Entrance Exam (ISEE). Some schools have their own examination that includes reading comprehension, essay writing, and mathematics for both elementary and secondary school students.

The selection of an independent school as the educational learning community of choice is not simply a parent or teacher decision—students often are also involved in the decision of selecting an independent school. The more personalized environment and the reputation of the school's success in preparing students for postsecondary education are reasons that students may select an independent rather than a public school for secondary education when they are provided this choice.

Social and economic diversity have been a priority for many independent schools. Many schools have established scholarships for minority and other children who would not be able to enroll without major financial support. There have been several programs established throughout the country to identify deserving students who are awarded full scholarships to independent schools. For instance, *A Better Chance* is a national program that identifies and recruits disadvantaged junior and high school students in private schools throughout the United States (A Better Chance, 2000). The program is designed to prepare their scholars to face the many challenges they may face in their new school environment and to provide ongoing support throughout their experience. Students are awarded need-based financial aid packages that may include scholarships, grants, and loans.

Faculty and Staff

Teachers select independent schools as places for employment for many of the same reasons that parents view these schools. In an age of urbanization and anonymity, teachers also seek the small school environment of the independent school as safer, more personalized, and a more positive work environment than public schools. In addition, many teachers view the less bureaucratic environment of the independent school as an opportunity for increased autonomy in the implementation and design of instructional practices. For example, Kane (1992a) reports that teachers select independent schools as sites for employment because of the personalized and family-like atmosphere wherein teachers are given freedom in choosing texts and curriculum, and students are perceived as motivated to learn. Teachers also recognize that increased parental involvement characterizes many independent schools. Teachers who are seeking a work environment in which parents are more actively engaged with the school in the joint responsibility of educating the child turn to independent schools for employment.

Federal and State Legislation

In 1925, in *Pierce v. Society of Sisters* (1925), the United States Supreme Court established that private school attendance would satisfy compulsory education requirements. This case also established that private schools have a right to engage in the business of education. Since that time, states have created statutes codifying that attendance at a nonpublic school satisfies compulsory education laws (Alexander & Alexander, 1998; LaMorte, 1999).

Independent schools have become self-sufficient organizations that are unwilling to be encumbered with local, state, or federal governmental regulations or monitoring; however, there are minimal state and local regulations governing them. Although state regulation of independent schools is minimal and varied, schools are required to accurately track and report student attendance, follow health and safety standards, and adhere to regulations concerning the number of school days. Schools are also required to meet state curricular and graduation standards (Alexander & Alexander, 1998; LaMorte, 1999).

Finance

As businesses, independent schools are "incorporated as not-for-profit, tax-exempt corporations. Independent schools rely primarily on tuition for support, supplemented by gifts from parents, alumni, foundations, corporations, and (for some) income from an endowment" (Kane, 1992b, p. 7). The cost for attending an independent school varies according to the type of school, location, age or grade level of the child, and the school's history and tradition. The price to attend a day school can range from $6,500–$20,000 per year; whereas, the cost for a boarding school can vary from $18,000–$30,000 per year. For instance, at one independent boarding school in the east, tuition, room, and board costs were $27,750 for boarding students during the 2000–2001 school year. This amount does not include books and supplies ($550), a health center fee ($150), a general fee ($525), and a technology fee ($730). Tuition for day students is $20,550 per year, and the general fee ($365), books and supplies ($550), and technology fee ($730) are additional (Northfield Mt. Hermon School, 2000).

Generally, scholarships, financial aid, and tuition waivers are available for students in many independent schools. In addition, policy debates continue in the political arena concerning vouchers for students to attend independent schools and tax credits for independent school tuition.

Accountability

Independent schools are market-driven. The tenets that are currently driving public school reform of excellence, accountability, and competition have always driven independent schools. Like any private business, independent schools must satisfy their customers who pay a great deal and may make personal financial sacrifices to have their children attend these schools. Besides achieving their philosophical and educational mission, independent schools must demonstrate that they provide quality education. This means that the schools must demonstrate that they are achieving their stated goals. Besides their students and parents, independent schools are accountable to the alumni, foundations, and corporations that provide continuous support. Many of the college preparatory independent schools consider that they are also accountable to colleges and universities that help them remain competitive. Independent schools, therefore, must demonstrate that they are achieving excellence, because they are accountable to their various constituencies who will not provide financial support in this very competitive climate.

In keeping with the desire to maintain high standards and be competitive in today's market-driven environment, seven regional associations accredit independent schools. These are the Middle States Association of Colleges and Schools (MSACS), the New England Association of Colleges and Schools (NEASC), the North Central Association of Colleges and Schools (NCACS), the Northwest Association of Schools and Colleges (NASC), the Southern Association of Colleges and Schools (SACS), and the Western Association of Schools and Colleges (WASC) (National Association of Independent Schools, 2001). Additionally, some regions and states have other independent school associations that sponsor evaluation and accreditation programs for member schools.

Advantages and Disadvantages

The advantages of independent schools include the variety of kinds of independent schools, making it therefore possible to find a school that meets the individual needs of the child; a competitive, market-driven structure leads to a reputation for high standards; active parent and alumni involvement in the life of the school; a large scholarship program; rich and diverse curriculum with strong arts, sports, and elective programs; outstanding facilities and state-of-the art technology; small class size and low teacher/student ratio; faculty that has tremendous autonomy in the classroom; minimal state and local control; and most graduates attending and graduating from college. Esty (1991) specifies the following advantages for students who choose independent schools: (1) attention to individual learning styles and rates, (2) teaching all the time, (3) athletics for everyone, (4) nurturing a sense of community service, (5) partnership and shared values with graduates and parents, (6) the potential to be in a multicultural community, and (7) teaching, learning, and living in an ethical context (pp. 488–489). Many private schools have marketed their institution's positive elements effectively to influence student selection of their school based on these features.

Even though independent schools are committed to social and economic diversity, occasionally a disadvantage for students can be the difficulty of adjusting to the academic and social environment. Additionally, the cost to attend independent schools is often prohibitive for many families; and schools must remain competitive or they will lose their students to other schools. Another disadvantage often perceived by the larger community is that independent schools draw selected "better" students away from the traditional neighborhood school, and are resistant to working with difficult or learning challenged students.

Summary

Although independent school growth has occurred in the last two decades, public schools outnumber independent schools in the United States (NAIS, 2000). As we continue in the 21st century, some issues that should be addressed regarding the future of independent schools include the need for an emphasis on (1) a continuing commitment to diversity, (2) attracting a higher caliber of teachers, (3) more choices in the types of curriculum, and (4) improving work conditions (Esty, Jr., 1991). Our nation's demographics are changing. In response to this change, it has become increasingly important for independent schools to educate diverse student populations. As our nation faces a growing teacher shortage, the need to recruit and retain high quality teachers in independent schools becomes a shared need of both public and independent schools. Independent schools must be proactive in designing outreach efforts, both to recruit a diverse student body and to recruit a high-quality teaching staff. Attention to maintaining a positive and productive environment is also important in retaining the needed teachers.

According to Levison (1994), independent schools share the same basic core technology of the classroom and student-teacher relationship. As all schools aim minimally to help students become proficient in the basics of reading, writing, and arithmetic, most share similar basic educational objectives as far as academic preparation or cognitive development of students is concerned. Independent schools do, however, differ from public schools. Although independent schools are diverse in their educational missions, they generally share six basic characteristics of "self-governance, self-support, self-defined curriculum, self-selected students, self-selected faculty, and small size" (Kane, 1992b, p. 397). The continued growth of independent schools may well depend on how effectively independent schools continue to market these features using the refinements of these characteristics as an opportunity for continual improvement.

Most schools that now call themselves independent were once satisfied to be called private, and the latter term is still widely used. The change to greater use of the term independent versus private schools has come about largely for two reasons: The first reason is because of dissatisfaction with the association with the concept of private ownership, which the term "private" suggests. The second reason for the term independent schools to be used instead of private schools is "because of dissatisfaction with the implication of exclusiveness of being called, in a sense, 'Private, Keep Out!'" (Potter, 1971, p. 18). Independent schools currently are seeking to become schools of choice for an increasingly diverse student body.

The most significant unique characteristic of the independent school "is its voluntary nature. It offers choice" (Kane, 1992b, p. 397). Just as the airlines who say, "We recognize you have a choice. Thank you for selecting us," therein lies the primary strength promulgated by independent schools today. Increasingly, parents, teachers, and students of diverse ethnic and socioeconomic backgrounds recognize that they do have a choice in selecting their educational environment. The future of independent schools will be influenced by the growing number of individuals who execute that choice and by the policymakers who lobby for change in the current public school system of education to open the avenue of choice to diverse populations of various socioeconomic groups.

Internet Sources

- *http://www.nais.org/*
  The National Association of Independent Schools' site that provides information about the organization and the services it provides. It has an extensive school, state, and regional association database. The site provides basic information about admissions and financial aid. The site has excellent links to other related independent school organizations such as the Southern Association of Independent Schools.

- *http://www.schools.com/*
  The Association of Boarding Schools is a nonprofit organization that serves over 300 boarding schools. The site provides extensive information about national and international schools, the admission

process, a copy of the common application used by all boarding schools, and information for international families.

- *http://www.ncgs.org/*
  The National Coalition of Girl's Schools is composed of the 91 members of the independent, parochial, and public girls' schools.

- *http://www.jbsa.org/*
  Junior Boarding Schools Association is a coalition of 14 schools that specifically cater to students in grades one to nine. The informative site provides information about boarding school life and provides a direct link to each of the member schools.

- *http://www.boysschoolscoalition.org/*
  The International Boys' Schools Coalition is an international advocacy organization of boy's schools with a listing of participating schools and a direct link to most.

- *http://www.capenet.org/*
  The Council for American Private Education is a coalition of 13 national organizations serving private elementary schools.

- *http://www.sais.org/about.htm*
  Southern Association of Independent Schools.

Chapter References

A Better Chance, I. (2000). *A Better Chance Homepage.* Author. [Online]. Available: *http://abetterchance.org/* [2001, May 25].

Alexander, K., & Alexander, M. D. (1998). *American Public School Law* (4th ed.). New York: West/Wadsworth Publishing Company.

Esty, Jr., J. C. (1991). Independent schools: what, whither, and why. *Teachers College Record*, 92, 488–489.

Kane, P. R. (1992a). What is an independent school? In P. R. Kane (Ed.), *Independent schools, independent thinkers* (pp. xxviii, 416). San Francisco: Jossey-Bass.

Kane, P. R. (1992b). Independent schools in American education. *Teachers College Press*, 92 (3), 396–498.

LaMorte, M. W. (1999). *School law: Cases and concepts* (6th ed.). Boston: Allyn & Bacon.

Levison, L. M. (1994). *Community service programs in independent schools.* New York: Garland Publishing, Inc.

National Association of Independent Schools [NAIS]. (2000). *NAIS Web Pages.* Author. Available: *http://www.nais.org/.*

Northfield Mt. Herman School. (2000). *Northfield Mt. Herman School Handbook.* Massachusetts.

Pierce v. Society of Sisters, 268 U.S. 510 (U.S. 1925).

Potter, C. (1971). The independent school. In G. Riemer, *How a private school can help your child* (p. 18). New York: Association Press.

Southern Association of Independent Schools. (2001). SAIS Web pages. Author. Available: *http://www.sais.org.*

Tauber, R. T. (1995). What can we learn from the marketing of independent schools. *NASSP Bulletin,* 90.

Unger, H. G. (1993). *How to pick a perfect private school.* New York: Facts on File.

Chapter Seven

Catholic Schools

Lenoar Foster, Ed.D.

The presence of Catholic schools can be traced back to America's colonial period. According to Bryk, Lee, and Holland (1993), "the development of schools in Catholic communities during this period closely paralleled activities occurring in Protestant communities. Education was viewed as a fundamentally moral enterprise, and Protestants and Catholics sought to ground the education of their children in their particular beliefs" (p. 18). Liberal arts colleges and secondary schools for boys grew from seminaries established to train Catholic clergy. Religious orders of women conducted academies for girls and, subsequently, sponsored free primary schools for poor children that they were able to establish from the tuition fees assessed to wealthy students attending their girls' academies. These primary schools for poor children became precursors to the "parochial schools" that came to be organized by Catholics around their parish churches (Bryk, Lee, & Holland, 1993; Seller, 1977). Saint Mary's Church in Philadelphia was the site of the first parish school of record in 1782 (Bryk, Lee, & Holland, 1993).

Another major catalyst for the continued development of parochial schools in the United States was the mass influx of immigrants to the United States during the early part of the 19th century. Many of these newly arrived immigrants were Catholics who came to view the common schools established during the 1830s and 1840s as being dominated by Protestant religious bodies that were blatantly anti-Catholic and pro-Protestant theology in their instructional methodologies and pedagogy.

In order to counter the rampant anti-Catholic and nativist sentiments pervading the public schools of the 19th century and to safeguard the religious education of their children, U.S. Catholics established a system of schools that sprang from the work of meetings of U.S. Catholic bishops in plenary councils held in Baltimore, Maryland, in 1852, 1866, and 1884. A central theme of these meetings of Catholic bishops was that "religious instruction should not be separated from other forms of instruction" (Spring, 1997, p. 83). Mandates of the U.S. bishops from the Third Plenary Council of 1884 established the system of Catholic schools in the United States. These mandates stipulated the following:

I. That near every church a parish school, where one does not yet exist, is to be built and maintained in perpetuum within two years of the promulgation of this council, unless the bishop should decide that because of serious difficulties a delay may be granted. . . .

IV. That all Catholic parents are bound to send their children to the parish school, unless it is evident that a sufficient training in religion is given either in their own homes, or in other Catholic schools; or when because of sufficient reason, approved by the Bishop, with all precautions and safeguards, it is licit to send them to other schools. What constitutes a Catholic school is left to the decision of the Bishop. (McCluskey, 1964, p. 94)

The creation and establishment of a system of Catholic schools by the Third Plenary Council of 1884 was "considered as beneficial to the state because such schools would create better citizens by creating better Christians" (Spring, 1997, p. 84). Choice and benefit played equal hands in the establishment of the system of Catholic schools that developed in this country from the 19th century to the present.

Structure

Catholic schools operate and are governed by the source of their sponsorship. The four classifications under which Catholic schools operate include:

- Parish: sponsored by a single parish church community
- Inter-parish: sponsored by two or more parishes
- Diocesan: sponsored by the archdiocese
- Private: sponsored by a religious order or a private corporation (McDonald, 2001, p. 9).

Organizationally, Catholic schools are structured as elementary, middle, and high schools. The elementary grades generally encompass grades 1 through 8. Middle schools encompass grades 6 through 8, and grades 9 through 12 constitute high schools. Increasingly, a number of Catholic schools have established preschool and kindergarten units within their elementary schools. Extended day programs, involving before-and/or after-school activities, were reported in 66.8% of Catholic elementary and middle schools during the 2000–2001 school year (McDonald, 2001, p.23).

In the academic year 2000–2001, there were 8,146 Catholic schools in the United States; 6,920 were elementary and middle schools, and 1,226 were secondary schools (McDonald, 2001, p. 6). The vast majority of Catholic elementary schools (99.1%) and secondary schools (64.1%) are coeducational. At the high school level, 14.8% of all Catholic high schools are all-male schools, and 21.1% are all-female schools (McDonald, 2001, p. 10).

Today, total student enrollment in Catholic schools numbers 2,647,301. Of this total student enrollment, 2,004,037 are enrolled in elementary/middle schools, and 643,264 are enrolled in secondary schools (McDonald, 2001, p. ix). Growing diversity in student ranks continues to be a hallmark of Catholic school enrollment. In fact, the enrollment of ethnic minority students in Catholic schools has more than doubled in the past 30 years. In the academic year 2000–2001, ethnic minority student enrollment accounted for 25.6% of total Catholic school enrollment. Of that total, 8% were African-American students, 3.9% were Asian American students, and Hispanic student enrollment was at 10.9% (McDonald, 2001, p. 16). Additionally, Catholic schools have been welcoming to large numbers of non-Catholic students who seek the educational values imparted through Catholic education. Non-Catholic student enrollment amounted to 13.6% of the total student enrollment in the academic year 2000–2001 (McDonald, 2001, p. 18). Nationally, Catholic schools enjoy an enviable student /teacher ratio of 16:1 (McDonald, 2001, p. 19).

Since their establishment in the United States, Catholic schools have been staffed predominantly by priests and religious brothers and sisters. Increasingly, as the numbers of religious staff have been depleted by social and ministerial changes, Catholic schools are being staffed by a majority of lay faculty members. In the academic year 2000–2001, total full-time teaching personnel in Catholic schools numbered 161,496. Of this number, 93.5% were lay teachers and 6.5% of teachers were priests, brothers, and sisters.

In dioceses where a number of Catholic schools exist, they are generally organized as a "school system" over which an appointed superintendent presides. Depending upon the number and types of schools, a diocesan office of schools can be as complex in its organization (e.g., superintendent, associate superintendents, business managers, curriculum coordinators/specialists, religious education directors, etc.) as any public school district office, depending on the kinds of services it provides to its schools and the number of services it must coordinate in a central fashion for the schools, or as simple as a three person office (superintendent and two support staff persons). Generally, diocesan offices of education will coordinate salary schedules, school calendars, state and regional accreditation processes, federal programs in which parochial schools participate, and provide general guidelines relative to the adherence to general principles of Catholic teaching to which the schools are bound.

Holland (1997) notes that, "Decisions concerning curricular organization, length of teaching day, modular or block schedule, co-curricular activities, parent programs, and fund-raising efforts, among others, are determined at the school level" (p. 26). The history, traditions, practices, and needs of schools in a diocese play an important role in determining the kind and type of central control exerted by a diocesan school office. What is clear is that pastors of parishes in which schools are located, local parish/diocesan school boards, boards of trustees, administrators, teachers, and alumni play important and varied roles in sustaining the operational life of Catholic schools. This involvement creates both a sense of community and ownership in the work of Catholic schools.

Financing/Legislation

Catholic schools are primarily supported through the payment of tuition and fees. In academic year 2000–2001, the average tuition for an elementary school student was $1,787 per year, and the median tuition for a high school freshman student was $4,300. Average tuition costs in the academic year 2000–2001 accounted for 63% of the actual costs per pupil for elementary students and 75% of the actual costs for high school students. For the academic year 2000–2001, 81% of elementary schools and 97% of secondary schools provided some form of tuition assistance and/or scholarship aid (McDonald, 2001, p. 15). In all Catholic schools the differential between per pupil costs and actual tuition is amassed through a variety of systematic and creative ways. These include financial grants from the parishes and dioceses in which the schools are located, contributed services by members of religious orders who staff the schools, and a wide array of ongoing institutional development projects and fund-raising programs.

Like other private schools in the United States, students and teachers in Catholic schools have been afforded opportunities to participate in a number of educational programs sponsored by state and federal governments. These programs include authorized educational programs under the Elementary and Secondary Education Act (ESEA), federal nutrition programs, and government-subsidized/free transportation to school. Participation in these various programs do not result in direct aid to Catholic schools. Funds from these programs/activities are allotted by the federal and state governments to public school districts and/or state departments of education who are responsible for making these programs available to eligible students, teachers, and other school personnel within their districts whether they are in attendance in public or private schools (U.S.Department of Education, 1996). Voucher programs in which parents can choose to send their children to Catholic schools through use of public funds have encountered legal challenges throughout the nation.

Accountability

Like their public school counterparts, Catholic schools are held to the same academic and athletic accreditation standards imposed by the states in which they are located and by the regional accrediting associations that accredit secondary schools throughout the nation. Since teacher certification is controlled by the state, teachers in Catholic schools must also adhere to teacher certification requirements in the states where they teach to instruct in academic subject areas. Additionally, Catholic school systems also require specialized accreditation of teachers in areas of religious instruction, theology, and marriage and family studies in order to promote their distinctive educational missions.

Advantages/Disadvantages

Building upon several decades of research on the effectiveness of Catholic schools (Bryk, Lee, & Holland, 1993; Coleman & Hoffer, 1987; Greeley, 1982; Marks & Lee, 1989), Holland (1997) has identified five organizational characteristics that appear to contribute to the success of educational efforts in Catholic schools. These include: (1) requiring a core academic curriculum for all students; (2) creating a learning community in which students, teachers, and parents are integrally involved; (3) small classes that create a sense of community; (4) a decentralized governance structure; and (5) an inspirational ideology that reflects a specific vision and values in which students are educated (pp. 24–26).

In general, the same basic academic goals are mapped out for all students in Catholic schools. While some tracking and ability grouping does exist within the curriculum, these structures ensure that all students meet the requirements of the core curriculum. School policies and available fiscal and human resources are organized to support the attainment of school-wide instructional goals.

The philosophy of Catholic schools underscores beliefs about what students should learn and how those who work with them in the learning enterprise should assist the process. Both curricular and cocurricular activities provide opportunities for student-teacher interactions that reinforce the connection between what is learned in the classroom, and how what is learned in the classroom should be used in real-life situations. Importantly, teachers are expected to engage students in worthwhile activities beyond the walls of the school so that they can immediately see the connections between what they learn and how what they learn can be used to the best benefits of themselves and the communities in which they will live and work as contributing, caring, and responsible adults. In many instances the vision and values foundational to Catholic education guide the kinds of activities in which teachers seek to enlarge the educational experiences and views of their students. Involvement in varied projects that aim to provide services to the wider community in which the school is located are prominent in the educational experiences of many Catholic school students. Many Catholic schools require that students complete "service hour" requirements as part of studying certain subjects and as requirements for graduation. Importantly, because students work closely together in both curricular and cocurricular activities, they develop close relational bonds that foster greater understanding, and "social mixing among students of different races and social classes" (Holland, 1997, p. 25). This enhances and supports a diverse educational experience.

A number of writers (Gittell, et al., 1972; Malen & Ogawa, 1988; Rogers & Chung, 1983) have argued persuasively that more site-based control of a school and its educational activities and decisions, and less interference from external bureaucratic structures, allows for greater input by those most closely connected to the educational enterprise and can result in more effective schooling. Holland (1997) observes that the "Catholic school system is in fact a loose federation of schools whose governance depends on the ownership, which is typically a parish, diocese or religious order. Catholic schools have operated on a school-based management model for many years" (p. 26).

For all of the success accorded to Catholic schools, there remains a lingering accusation that such schools have high success rates because of "selection bias." That is, Catholic schools can be and are selective about the types of students they choose to admit, and are pretty narrow and subscribed in the curriculum they offer to the majority of students. As such, Catholic schools can admit only those students who can pay the tuition bill, can admit only those students who show promise of academic potential, and can dismiss those students who break rules and fail to live up to academic promise. Thus, according to many public school defenders, comparisons between Catholic schools and public schools become an unfair measure, since public schools must accommodate all students.

In the face of "selection bias," Stanfield (1997) has observed, despite accounting for selection bias that some researchers have attempted to adjust, that there still exists a 26% difference in the drop-out rate for minorities attending public and Catholic schools in inner cities; that large numbers of poor students do attend Catholic schools because tuition rates are relatively low, or have been adjusted to accommodate the financial contribution that poor families can contribute to the education of their students; that the vast majority of Catholic schools have not dismissed large numbers of students for a variety of academic failures and disciplinary infractions; that the structure and discipline accorded by Catholic schools to foster academic success are factors that are embraced by families, regardless of geography, race, or socioeconomic class, who choose to send their students to Catholic schools; and that recent court decisions that have favored public education services being delivered to students who attend Catholic schools have actually increased the diversity of student enrollment in Catholic schools. What researchers say accounts for the success of Catholic schools amid accusations of selection bias is the environment of high expectations and high standards that pervade the educational process and the preconditions of order and discipline that facilitate and encourage high achievements (Baker, Han, & Broughman, 1996; Bryk, Lee, & Holland, 1993; Holland, 1997).

Currently, students in Catholic schools constitute 50% of students who attend private schools (Most U.S. Private Schools Are Religious, 1999). Nonetheless, enrollment in Catholic schools has declined by 50% since 1965. According to Holland (1997), this decline has resulted "in a third fewer schools" (p. 24). Russo and Rogus (1998) have attributed the decline in student enrollment in Catholic schools to "a sharply diminished birthrate, migration of Catholic families to areas where Catholic schools were not available, the increasing costs of Catholic schooling, greater acceptance of public schools by Catholic parents and social attitudes" (p. 14).

The declining number of religious priests, brothers, and sisters who have traditionally staffed Catholic schools has contributed to lay people dominating the faculties of schools and to their increased costs as well (Russo & Rogus, 1998). Holland (1997) has observed that "new Catholic schools have not been established in suburbs where Catholic families have moved . . . Less than 2½ percent of existing Catholic schools were founded since 1980" (p. 24). Interestingly, as traditional Catholic families have migrated to the suburban areas, leaving their schools in old neighborhoods now occupied by increasing numbers of minority populations and non-Catholics, enrollment in many Catholic schools is becoming increasingly dominated by large numbers of non-Catholics and minority groups.

The changing demographics of Catholic schools present challenges that must be addressed if these institutions are to remain loyal to their traditional purposes and viable for serving a variety of functions that enhance and strengthen the educational learning base for both Catholic and large numbers of non-Catholic students who attend them. Russo and Rogus (1998) have outlined six related challenges that must receive attention: (1) Catholic schools must take great care in defining and maintaining their Catholic character and identity in the face of increasing non-Catholic enrollments; (2) Catholic schools must remain affordable institutions without excluding students from less fortunate means and backgrounds—on the other hand, Catholic leaders must continually strive to afford equitable salaries and benefits to faculties and staffs, most of whom are predominantly lay people, working in Catholic schools; (3) Catholic schools must maintain high academic standards while accomplishing the primary goal of providing a religious education and formation to the next generation of Catholics; (4) Catholic schools must identify and recruit future educational leaders for the schools; (5) Catholic schools must formulate means by which to educate large numbers of students from diverse economic, cultural, religious, ethnic, and racial backgrounds and still maintain a commitment to educate all children, including disabled students; and (6) Catholic schools must be committed to those practices and structures that have assured excellence but should also be open to experimentation, innovation, risk-taking, collaboration, and collegial working relations with external agencies and publics that will assure continuous improvement for the schools.

Conclusion

In highlighting the overall effectiveness of Catholic parochial schools, Robert Kealey of the National Catholic Education Association says it best: "Our teachers have a strong belief that every child can learn. No matter who the child is, no matter what the problems are at home, no matter what—that child can learn and that child will learn." (Kealey, quoted in Stanfield, 1997, p. 1646). Indeed, in taking this approach to educational attainment, Catholic schools embody the best "can-do" attitude that Americans have traditionally come to expect from their educational institutions. The success of students in Catholic schools can be linked to an unerring adherence to "high standards and high expectations for all students; a safe, disciplined, and highly structured environment; caring teachers who reach out and involve parents; a core curriculum that emphasizes the academic basics of reading, writing, mathematics, and science; and clear reciprocal responsibilities between school and home" (Stanfield, 1997, p. 1644).

Research on the effectiveness of Catholic schools has been consistent in three major findings: (1) students in Catholic schools outperform their public school counterparts in academic achievement; (2) Catholic schools have greater success with students from disadvantaged educational environments; and (3) a strong learning community supported by a clear sense of mission and core benchmarks for educational attainment correlate highly with the success that students experience (Bryk, Lee, & Holland, 1993; Holland, 1997; Russo & Rogus, 1998; Stanfield, 1997).

As the following true scenario illustrates, Catholic schools continue to contribute to a strong sense of community. It was graduation day, 1992—Saturday morning at about 9:30 A.M. Graduation would take place at 10:00 A.M. in the high school gymnasium. Brother Ignatius, a long time faculty member and principal of Bishop Manogue High School, noticed with pride the procession of cars and groups entering the campus for the annual graduation ceremony. The graduating class of 1992 numbered 200 students. Already, the gymnasium was filling, and it was obvious that some people attending the graduation ceremony would have to stand during the ceremony. Some families had arrived as early as 8:00 A.M. to stake out seating spaces for the members of their family—family members that included parents, siblings, grandparents from both sides of the families, godparents, neighbors, and members of the previous graduating class who had strong friendships with members of the class of 1992.

As Brother Ignatius brought himself back to the impending moment of graduation while returning to the main building, he noticed a solitary figure reflected against the backdrop of the outdoor student lounge area. The figure was Dick Arden, a 1959 graduate of the school. For as long as Brother Ignatius could remember Dick Arden and his wife, Ruth, has always been familiar faces at booster fund-raisers and at various academic, athletic, and social events during the school year.

Brother Ignatius greeted Dick and congratulated him and his wife on the graduation of their last child, Jimmy, from the school. Jimmy had been preceded in graduation by his four sisters—Cathy, Teresa, Suzy, and Jennifer. All of them, along with a host of relatives and friends from near and far, were present this day to witness the end of the Arden era at the school. Dick commented to Brother Ignatius about how much the school had meant and contributed to both his own personal development and that of his children. His eyes were teary, but his voice resonated with a pride borne of loyalty to an institution that was an integral part of his family's life. As the music signaled the beginning of the march of graduates, Dick turned to head toward the gymnasium. He turned to Brother Ignatius in a final comment and stated emphatically, "The Ardens are gone for a short period now, but we're looking forward to the years when our grandchildren will call this place home too. By the way, don't forget to keep me on the school newsletter and athletic events schedule, and I do plan to help with the school fundraiser next year. See you next year."

Internet Resources

For more information about Catholic education and educational opportunities in Catholic schools, please consult the following Internet sites:

- *http://www.ncea.org/*
  National Catholic Education Association (NCEA)—Organization for Catholic educators in the United States. Source for publications, events, general information on Catholic education, job listings, and other pertinent links.

- *http://www.ncea.org/About/briefhist.shtml*
  Brief History of the National Catholic Educational Association— Organizational chart, constitution of the association, board of directors

- *http://www.ncea.org/Elem*
  NCEA Elementary Schools Department

- *http://www.ncea.org/Scndry*
  Department of Secondary Schools

- *http://www.ncea.org/Boards*
  National Association of Boards, Councils, and Commissions of
  Catholic Education—Informative newsletter available.

- *http://www.ncea.org/Member*
  Membership in the National Catholic Educational Association.
  Membership services and benefits.

- *http://www.ncea.org/ReadRoom/momentum.shtml*
  Momentum: Journal of the National Catholic Educational Association

- *http://www.ncea.org/ReadRoom/momentum.shtml*
  Official award-winning publication of the National Catholic Educational Association.

- *http://www.ncea.org/PubPol*
  Public Policy Information and NCEA
  Federal programs, school choice initiatives, and U.S. Supreme Court
  decisions.

- *http://www.ncea.org/Admin/research.shtml*
  The National Center for Research in Catholic Education

Chapter References

Baker, D., Han, M., & Broughman, S. P. (1996). *How different, how similar? Comparing key organizational qualities of American public and private secondary schools.* Washington, DC: U.S. Department of Education, National Center for Education Statistics (NCES 96-322).

Bryk, A. S., Lee, V. E., & Holland, P. B. (1993). *Catholic schools and the common good.* Cambridge, MA: Harvard University Press.

Coleman, J. S., & Hoffer, J. (1987). *Public and private high schools: The impact of communities.* New York: Basic Books.

Gittell, M., Berube, M. R., Gottfried, F., Guttentag, M., & Spier, A. (1972). *Local control in education: Three demonstration school districts in New York City.* New York: Praeger Publishers.

Greeley, A. M. (1982). *Catholic high schools and minority students.* New Brunswick, NJ: Transaction Books.

Holland, P. B. (1997). Catholic school lessons for the public schools. *The School Administrator*, 54 (7), 24–25.

Malen, B., & Ogawa, R. T. (1988). Professional patron influence on site-based governance councils: A confronting case study. *Educational Evaluation and Policy Analysis*, 10, 251–270.

Marks, H. M., & Lee, V. E. (1989). *National assessment of educational proficiency in reading, 1985–1986: Catholic and public schools compared*. Washington, DC: National Catholic Education Association.

Most U.S. Private Schools Are Religious (1999). *CQ Researcher*, 9(13), 284.

McCluskey, N. (Ed.) (1964). *Catholic education in America: A documentary history*. New York: Teachers College Press.

McDonald, Dale (2001). *United States Catholic and elementary and secondary school, 2000–2001*. Washington, DC: National Catholic Educational Association.

Rogers, D., & Chung, N. H. (1983). *110 Livingston Street revisited: Decentralization in action*. New York: SUNY University Press.

Russo, C. J., & Rogus, J. F. (1998). Catholic schools: Proud past, promising future. *School Business Affairs*, 64 (6), 13–16.

Seller, M. (1977). *To seek America: History of ethnic life in the United States*. Englewood, NJ: Jerome S. Ozer, Publisher.

Spring, J. (1997). *The American school, 1642–1999* (4th ed.). New York: McGraw-Hill.

Stanfield, R. L. (1997). Answered prayers. *National Journal*, 29 (33), 1644–1646.

U.S. Department of Education (1996). *Serving private school students with federal education programs: A handbook for public and private school educators*. Washington, DC: U.S. Department of Education, Office of Non-Public Education.

Chapter Eight

Christian Schools

John Gooden, Ed.D.
C. Michelle Hooper, Ph.D.
Garth Petrie, Ed.D.

In the United States, school choice dates back to the beginning of public education. Parents have always had the option to decide how their children would be educated. In fact, this right was legally established in the 1925 landmark Supreme Court decision, *Pierce v. Society of Sisters*. The case established that parents have a Fourteenth Amendment liberty interest to decide how their children are educated without undue interference from state governments. Moreover, the court stated that private schools had a property right to exist and function. Now parents may choose to enroll their children in public, private, or parochial schools, or they may elect to homeschool them (Pierce, 1925).

According to the National Center for Education Statistics (1994), Christian schools are the second largest category of private or parochial schools; second only to Catholic schools. Today, Christian schools claim to have over 66,590 schools nationally and internationally. These faith-based schools first emerged during the 1950s in response to a growing dissatisfaction with public education. Initially, they were a part of a grassroots movement that was scattered and powerless; however, as dissatisfaction continued to grow, its members became more organized and increasingly more vocal during the 1960s and 1970s (McLaughlin, 1997).

Christian schools are typically interdenominational, Protestant, and represent a range of Christian evangelical groups, which are sometimes called fundamentalists and/or charismatic. Generally, what Christian school proponents have in common is their belief that Jesus Christ is their personal savior, that the Bible is God's creation and He speaks to them through it, that one must have a conversion experience to be "saved," and that spreading the teachings of the Bible and converting others to Christ is essential to their faith and their schools (Rose, 1993).

Nearly all Protestant denominations have Christian schools of some type. However, the three that are most involved in such programs are the Lutherans in the north-central states, the Baptists in the southern states, and the Seventh-Day Adventists in the northeast. The Full Gospel and the Pentecostal denominations are also represented with many schools but have less organized school systems. Much growth in the number of Christian schools has occurred within the past 10 years. For example, according to John R. Chandler, executive director of the Southern Baptist Association of Christian Schools, in 1992, there were 435 Southern Baptist schools. In 2001, there were 607 Southern Baptist schools in 34 states, enrolling a range of students from 17 in the smallest school to 1,204 students enrolled in the largest school (e-mail communication May 11, 2001).

Three major Christian school associations were instrumental in the development of these schools. The American Association Christian School (AACS), established in 1972, serves "over 210,000 students and teachers enrolled in approximately 1200 member schools" (AACS, 2000, p. 1). The Association of Christian Schools International (ACSI), established in 1978, serves "5,000 member schools from 115 countries with an enrollment of 1,030,000" (ACSI, 2000, p. 2). The Dutch Calvinist Church established Christian Schools International (CSI0) in 1920 and represents over 475 schools and enrolls 1000,000 students (Christian Schools International, 2000). These associations provide the following services to their memberships: monitoring and lobbying federal and state legislation; legal representation; school accreditation; staff development activities; teacher placement; insurance packages; providing national Bible, athletics, debate, and music competitions (Rose, 1993).

The growth of Christian schools throughout the United States was a widespread succession from public schools because they opposed the concepts of secular humanism, and values clarification in public schools (Rose, 1993). Besides emphasizing the basics, Christian schools provide "holistic, authoritative, closely disciplined, and God-centered education that emphasizes character development and spiritual training" (p. 456).

Structure

Organizational

Although Christian schools are located in every one of the 50 states, the heaviest concentration, according to a study completed by the National Center for

Education Statistics (1994), can be found in the south. Student enrollments for 90% of the schools surveyed have less than 300 children. Most are
coeducational, diverse, and are combined elementary and secondary
schools. The typical class size for 34% of the schools is 15, and the student-
teacher ration is 14:1. Many parents approve of this small class size and the
student-teacher ratio, believing their children gain valuable assistant in their
learning.

McLaughlin (1997) reports that only 14% of Christian school teachers surveyed did not have a bachelor's degree, and 20% have advanced degrees.
However, this varies with the school and the curriculum being followed.

Fifty-eight percent of Christian schools reported that state certification is
not a widely utilized criteria for teacher employment. Regarding administrators, 87% of principals have 10 or more years of experience, and 50% have advanced degrees. Both teachers and administrators are paid less than those in
similar positions in other private schools and benefit plans are smaller; however, the majority of Christian school faculty are satisfied with their salaries,
class size, and staff cooperation. Student violence, racial tension, and poverty
are viewed as problems only by a limited number within the population. However, teachers do indicate that they have very little control over class content
and choice of textbooks (McLaughlin, 1997; Rose, 1993).

Curricula

Although the most significant factor influencing the structure of a Christian
school may be the management style of the individuals involved and the
doctrinal influences of the affiliated church (personal communication, ACSI
representative, 2001), the use of a solitary curriculum greatly impacts the culture of these schools. In fact, the structure of a Christian school is often
determined, in part, by the nature of its adopted curriculum. Choices available
for Christian education include prepackaged materials designed for a self-
paced educational environment, textbooks for use in a traditional classroom setting, as well as copies of primary source documents. Not all schools
adopt a specific program in its entirety. There are several private Christian
schools that elect to "pick and choose" their curriculum materials, and what
they choose is not always Christian-based. Secular programs, such as Saxon
Math, Bloomenfeld (math), the Shirley Method (English), and the Spalding
Method (phonics), can be found in a variety of evangelical Christian education
settings.

Although there are several Christian-based curricula used in many of today's evangelical Christian schools, three of the best known are School of Tomorrow, A Beka Books, and The Principle Approach. Descriptions of these curricula follow:

1. School of Tomorrow

    The *School of Tomorrow* curriculum is a prepackaged educational program designed by Accelerated Christian Education, Inc. (ACE). According to their promotional literature, *School of Tomorrow* is based on five fundamental principles of learning (*School of Tomorrow*, 2001, p. 2). These include: (1) instructing students at levels where they can perform; (2) setting reasonable goals; (3) controlling and motivating students; (4) measuring learning; and (5) rewarding learning.

    Each school that contracts with ACE must have a governing board that agrees to follow the basic premise of the program. *School of Tomorrow* offers individualized instruction in the form of a Packet of Accelerated Christian Education (PACE), which divides subject matter normally housed in one textbook into separate workbooks. Each grade level contains 12 PACES per subject, and students may not advance to the next PACE until mastery is demonstrated. If an area of weakness is detected, filler PACES are prescribed for remediation. Biblical values and character traits are integrated throughout the curriculum.

    Due to their focus on individualized study, schools using the *School of Tomorrow* curriculum do not provide teacher-led instruction. Rather, students work independently in cubicles, with supervisors and monitors available to answer questions (School of Tomorrow, 2001).

2. A Beka Book

    Administrators at Pensacola Christian College in Pensacola, Florida, developed the *A Beka Book* academic program. Their "formula for success," according to their Web site mission statement, describes *A Beka Books* as a "treasury of textbooks and teaching materials that reflect the very best in scholarship design, practicality, and Scriptural fidelity for academic excellence and good character training" (A Beka Books, 2001, p. 1).

    The *A Beka Books* curriculum is designed for use in schools with a traditional approach to classroom teaching. Training sessions are held regularly at the program's headquarters in Florida to acquaint teachers and administrators with the curriculum. *A Beka Books* provides their own textbooks that are written and developed by Christian scholars who, according to the program's literature, are also familiar with aspects of classroom instruction.

3. The Principle Approach

    This curriculum, which takes a classical Christian approach to learning, was developed by the Foundation for American Christian Education (F.A.C.E.). The Principle Approach offers an array of K–12 materials, including primary source documents in literature, government, history, and French. The teachers themselves, however, write the majority of the curriculum. A cornerstone of the program is the use of the 1828 edition of *Webster's American Dictionary of the English Language*, which was written from a Christian perspective. F.A.C.E. discourages the use of more modern dictionaries due to their secularized nature.

    Integrated into the Principle Approach is *The Noah Plan*. Named for Noah Webster, this philosophy views education in the tradition of the American Founding Fathers by focusing on what F.A.C.E. deems the "Four R" (reasoning, reflection, relating, and recording) of education. Students are encouraged to research primary American governmental documents and the Holy Bible to better understand their Christian heritage (The Noah Plan Classical Education Curriculum, 2000, pp. 3–5).

Financing

Christian schools are generally financed by tuition; however, 96% offer discounts and, overall, the tuition is significantly lower than that of other private schools. Only two percent of the elementary schools and 8% of the secondary schools charge tuition that is more than $3,500 a year (NCES, 1997). Some Christian schools are also aided by minimal financial support from local churches and school fund-raising activities. Many, if not most, buildings that house the schools are provided by the local church that sponsors them. Their political activism has also benefitted the schools financially over the years, and they have amassed an impressive array of public policies in their favor. Some of these policies include tax-free status; services under Title I (Chapter I) of the new Education Consolidation and Improvement Act, which allow state governments to fund private schools directly should local school boards refuse to grant them educational services guaranteed under the law; and aid under categorical programs such as special education. One of the most important political victories has been the legal precedent set by the Supreme Court decision in *Mueller v. Allen* (463 U.S. 388, 1983), which affirmed, as constitutional, the tax deduction plan in Minnesota allowing parents who send their children to private schools to claim a deduction on their state income tax (Rose, 1993).

Federal and State Legislation

The battle for support of private Christian schools has been one-sided throughout the history of education in the United States. Invariably, the federal courts have ruled for the separation of church and state, ultimately leaving Christian education to fend for itself through tuition and local church support. However, recent events indicate the tide may be turning toward a more equitable climate for these schools. For example, the tax deduction plan mentioned earlier in Minnesota allows a state tax deduction that indicates an indirect form of state support for private education.

Other federal legislation has also provided relief for certain categories of students, such as those with special education needs through Title One funds. Most recently, the Bush administration has highlighted some changes that focus on a controversial voucher system that ideally would, if enacted, provide funding that would follow the child, rather than be assigned to a particular category of school. Of course, in the spring 2001, session of Congress, voucher programs were written out of the educational reforms passed.

Accountability

Accountability is generally accomplished for schools through private organizations and national, state, and local agencies that monitor a particular organization or school. However, many Christian Schools believe that they ultimately answer only to the tenets of their faith, and all else is secondary. In fact, according to Sandy Mossman, a customer service representative for the *School of Tomorrow*, many *School of Tomorrow* learning centers are not accredited because the school is an extension of a church ministry and does not want an outside agency giving its approval to what they view as God's work. They want to remain autonomous, and fear if their Monday school is subject to approval, how far behind is their Sunday school?

Certainly, Christian schools are accountable to their various constituent groups (parents, teachers, and students), and if these groups are not satisfied with the way the school is achieving its mission and goal, parents will remove their children and teachers will find positions elsewhere (Harris, 2001). While Christian schools are accountable for academic excellence, many supporters consider that they are held to a higher standard than public schools because they are a faith-based community.

While some state accrediting agencies accredit private schools, some, like Texas's, do not. Instead, Texas has created an accrediting approval group called Texas Private School Accreditation Commission (TEPSAC). TEPSAC serves as a bridge between approved accrediting groups, such as ACSI, and the state Texas Education Agency (TEA) and offers state recognition to Christian schools accredited by agencies that are members of TEPSAC (Harris, 2001). Each of the national Christian school associations, The Association of Christian Schools International (ACSI), the American Association of Christian Schools (AACS), and Christian Schools International (CSI), offers accreditation through their organizations. However, some Christian schools elect to be accredited also by state and regional organizations, such as SACS (Southern Association of Colleges and Schools).

Accreditation is an area that parents, as well as faculty, should closely examine. For example, according to one accreditation representative, there are many "bogus" for-profit accreditation agencies that exist primarily to certify schools, for a fee (Personal communication, ACSI representative). These stamps of approval are often meaningless to college and university admissions offices. Additionally, students exiting a nonaccredited program or a program whose accreditation status is not recognized by the public schools may be required by their college of choice to pass additional entrance exams prior to admittance (Harris, 2001).

In response to the high stakes testing climate of the United States, most Christian Although every school differs in the academic testing requirement of its students, most Christian schools test their students annually with a nationally normed standardized test, such as the Stanford Achievement Test or the Iowa Test of Basic Skills (Harris, 2001). Generally, high school students are encouraged to participate in the Scholastic Aptitude Test (SAT) and the American College Testing Assessment (ACT) also. In Texas, for example, public school students are mandated to participate in a state-wide testing program, the Texas Assessment of Academic Skills. At this time, Christian schools may participate in this testing, but are not mandated to do so (2001).

Advantages and Disadvantages

Advantages of Christian schools include the opportunity for some students to work within a self-paced curriculum, a setting of small school size, and an education program that openly integrates biblical truths with daily instruction and, generally, active parent involvement. Another frequently mentioned advantage of Christian schools is the likelihood of a strong value agreement between parents, faculty, and students (Harris, 2000).

Disadvantages include the possibility that a school may not be accredited, which in some cases could affect college admissions. Additionally, in some states, faculty do not receive credit for years of service in nonaccredited institutions should they move to the public sector. Unlike ACSI, which requires that all of its accredited schools hire certified or degreed teachers, some Christian school programs are not required to hire credentialed faculty. While the small size school and class size may be considered an advantage, it also may be a disadvantage, especially at the high school level, where course offerings are limited due to fewer faculty.

Summary

Parents who choose to place their children in private Christ-centered education are often seeking a safe, drug-free environment that promotes a Christian worldview (Appleby, 1989). Others pursue Christian education to avoid what they perceive as too much governmental interference in their children's education. Those who focus on the religious instruction provided in Christian schools often cite Scriptures from the Holy Bible to support their decision. For example, Proverbs 2:6, in the King James Version, states, "For the Lord giveth wisdom: out of his mouth cometh knowledge and understanding."

Other parents who elect to place their children in Christian schools are looking for self-paced curriculum programs that emphasize character development as well as academics. One parent of a *School of Tomorrow* student emphasized that her son "finished high school in three years and, then, completed college in three years." Another parent commented that her son was able to be "self-paced in his curriculum. He is allowed to continue in areas that he grasps easily, is given extra time with things he does not understand and his progress is monitored so that no subject is overlooked."

Another parent commented that her son learned "how to think and reason, not just recite information." This parent liked the commitment to essay testing and competition provided in the Christian school her son attended. An ACSI representative pointed out that Christian schools offer the "best alternative for teaching the truth. They provide an opportunity to teach not just academics but also spiritual principles, and reinforce what is taught at home. There is a school-church-home triad."

Do Christian schools provide a better education than public schools? There is no conclusive proof of that fact if one is speaking of academic worth. However, if one is asking about religious growth and knowledge, the answer seems quite clear. Public schools have been controlled in their teaching in this area by laws and court decisions.

Parents and educators need to carefully define what they want for their children and themselves while remembering the biblical admonition of "in the world but not of the world." All individuals interested in Christian schools should ask these questions:

1. For what purpose is this school preparing students?

2. How does this school offer instruction? In secluded carrels or in open classrooms?

3. How well prepared are teachers for teaching?

4. How certified is the school for advancement to a university?

Internet Resources

Each of the websites identified below list member schools, outline services, highlight publications and resources, have job databases, and provide listings of their various state associations.

- *http://www.gospel.com/net/csi/*
  Christian Schools International

- *http://www.acsi.org/*
  Association of Christian Schools International

- *http://www.aacs.org/*
  American Association of Christian Schools

- *http://www.schooloftomorrow.com*
  School of Tomorrow

- *http://www.face.net/*
  The Principle Approach

- *http://www.abeka.com*
  A Beka Book

Chapter References

A Beka Books. (2001). Our foundation: The principles and precepts of God's word. [On-line]. Available: http://www.abeka.com/ABB/Catalogs/AboutABA/foundation .html.

American Association of Christian Schools (AACS) (2000). *American Association of Christian Schools Homepage.* Author. Available: *http://www.aacs.org/.*

Appleby, R. S. (1989). Keeping them out of the hands of the state: Two critiques of Christian Schools. *American Journal of Education, 98* (1), 62–82.

Association of Christian Schools International [ACSI] (2000). *Christian Schools International Homepage.* Author. Available: *http://www.gospelcom.net/csi/.*

Christian Schools International [CSI] (2000). *Christian Schools International Homepage.* Author. Available: *http://www.gospel.com/net/csi.*

Harris, S. (2000). A comparison of public and private school teachers' job satisfaction. Unpublished raw data.

Harris, S. (2001). One private school's response to educational standards. In R. Horn & J. Kincheloe (Eds.), *American Standards: Quality education in a complex world: The Texas case* (pp. 320–328). New York: Peter Lang.

McLaughlin, D. H. (1997). *Private schools in the United States a statistical profile, 1993–94* [microform 1 v]. Washington, DC: U.S. Dept. of Education Office of Educational Research and Improvement Educational Resources Information Center: National Center for Education Statistics.

Pierce v. Society of Sisters, 268 U.S. 510 (1925).

Rose, S. (1993). Christian fundamentalism and education in the United States. In M. E. Marty & R. S. Appleby (Eds.), *Fundamentalism and Society: Reclaiming the sciences, the family, and education* (Vol. 2, pp. 452–489). Chicago: The University of Chicago Press.

School of Tomorrow. (2001). School of Tomorrow in a nutshell. School of Tomorrow Web page. [On-line]. Available: http://www.schooloftomorrow.com/.

The Noah Plan Classical Education Curriculum. (2001). The Noah Plan: A complete classical and Biblical curriculum. Web page. [On-line]. Available: http:// www.face.net/Noah_plan.html.

Chapter Nine

Homeschools

Sharon Spall, Ph.D.
Brian Kasperitis

Introduction

Increased numbers of parents are withdrawing their children from private and public schools to school at home (Lines, 2000b). At such a time, the parent steps into a role of higher involvement than ever before in the academic and social development of his/her child (Hill, 2000). The decision to homeschool is an investment of time and resources and a decision that often invokes criticism from family and friends as well as from educators. There are those who question the academic rigor of home schooling and the self-interest of homeschooling parents, which these critics call a lack of regard for principles basic to a democratic society (Apple, 2000; Kohn, 1998; Lubienski, 2000;).

Homeschooling is education that is parent directed and that takes place in the student's home during the conventional school days of the week and may occur at all grade levels (Ray, 2000). Parents who homeschool represent most racial and income groups (Aizenman, 2000; McDowell, Sanchez, & Jones, 2000; Kleiner, 2000; Ray, 2000), but the majority appear to be from white middle- and upper-middle income groups (McDowell et. al, 2000). There is general agreement in the literature that the teacher parent is usually the mother, McDowell, 2000). Although accurate data on the exact number of homeschooled children is not available, the estimated number by researchers is over a million and growing. The exact number of parents and children homeschooling in the United States cannot be determined, because some states require parents to register in order to homeschool and some do not. Parents who read articles that attempt to generalize research findings to all homeschooling parents and all homeschooled children, or read reports that compare homeschool students with public school students, should be cautioned because the composition of the sample of such studies may be biased.

Obviously, bias raises internal validity issues and weakens the claims put forth in the research. Often, samples for research studies on homeschooling have been drawn from groups of parents and students who contract with a private test service or from groups entering Christian universities (Lines, 2000a; Rudner, 1998; Ray, 2000; Welner & Welner, 1999). Although these studies describe the sample well, the results are not generalizable to all homeschooled students or comparable to public school students (Hill, 2000). Of the students studied, the academic achievement and social maturity do not appear to be hurt by parents teaching at home (Lines, 2000a; Ray, 2000; Rudner, 1998).

The samples described in homeschool studies do not indicate that all parents are certified teachers. The courts have pointed out that private schools are recognized alternatives to public schooling, and teachers do not have to be certified, and such consideration is extended to homeschooling. Although some parents have college degrees and some are teachers, not all parents are educated above the high school level (Ray, 2000).

The reasons that parents decide to homeschool may vary. The primary reasons appear to center on academic and ideological concerns (Taylor, 1997), and these parents state dissatisfaction with what is taught and how the content is delivered. More specifically, parents complain that behavioral and academic standards are low. Many parents who prefer a religious based curriculum complain that the public school represents only the secular world (Carper, 2000). This differs somewhat in isolated rural regions where parents prefer to teach at home rather than submit children to long travel times or boarding school (Sherwood, 1989). Students with special needs, such as a child with a learning disability, or a gifted child, are found in the homeschool populations (Ensign, 2000). Parents of minority groups are concerned that racism is on the increase in the schools and do not want their children subjected to unkind treatment by teachers or other students (Ray, 2000). In some cases, parents turn to home teaching when the curriculum is not challenging or the formal public or private school classroom does not emphasize the strengths of the child. Parents also complain about the poor communication from the school and about the bureaucratic structure of both private and public schools that put parents on the outside, that restrict the flow of information, and that stifle collaboration with the home.

The problems with the organized, formalized school cause parents to recognize the benefits of homeschooling. Ray (2000) points out that the homeschool setting provides a learning environment that considers the primary factors associated with increased achievement. Individualized curriculum, increased and immediate feedback to students and parents, possibility of direct instruction on a greatly reduced class size (one-on-one), opportunities to easily implement mastery learning, opportunities to contextualize all learning on an individual basis and link the home and the community, and increased parent involvement are cited as important in all learning situations, but are present by the very nature of homeschooling. Parents can design a flexible learning plan that fits the family and the child.

Legislation and Accountability

During the 1970s and 1980s, school officials and homeschooling parents were confronted by public school officials and state authorities who legally and politically maneuvered to keep children in schools under the compulsory attendance laws. Between the 1970s and the mid 1990s, the relationship between homeschooling parents and public school officials has evolved from hostility to tolerance and sometimes even cooperation (Crowson, 2000). Present-day homeschooling benefits from those early days of confrontation resulted in legislation that recognizes homeschooling as an alternative to public school attendance (Lines, 2000a; 2000b). Five factors appear to determine the nature of the homeschool of today (McDowell & Ray, 2000). These five factors are: state legislation, religious organizations, educational institutions, technology, and the parent.

By 1970, all states in the United States had enacted compulsory attendance laws for public education except Mississippi, which followed in 1983. However, not until 1986 was homeschooling legally allowed in all 50 states. Each state has unique regulations, and parents are accountable for the regulations of the state laws. The Home School Legal Assistance Web site summarizes the legal stance of every state and the methods of compliance in that state. Some states require instruction in specified curriculum areas, state registration for homeschooling, and/or testing at specified times. Other states simply list homeschooling as an alternative to public school attendance.

In addition to state statues that allow homeschooling, the courts have held that proof of adequate instruction is the responsibility of the state. Alexander and Alexander (2001) explain the position of the state in the following quote:

> In summary, if a state statute allows for home instruction as an alternative to compulsory attendance, the burden falls on the state to show that the parent is not, in fact, providing such instruction. If the state has set out few standards governing home instruction, the inadequacy of such instruction may be diffi-

cult to prove. The state must produce evidence documenting the parent's fail-
ure to furnish adequate home instruction, and the parent must respond to
such evidence. However, the final burden of proof rest on the state to show that
the instruction failed to meet state requirements (p. 257).

The parent considering homeschooling as an option to public or private
school attendance must contact a state official for the standards and accountability procedures for homeschooling (Hill, 2000). State laws vary greatly
from one state to another. The parent must know the acceptable ways these
standards are met or, in other words, how the state holds the parent accountable. If a state can prove inadequate instruction as indicated in the statute, the
parent will have to respond to the evidence. In recent years, court cases regarding homeschooling are rare; those that do occur usually involve the regulation of homeschool (to determine if the parent is complying with state)
and not the right to homeschool (Ishizuka, 2000).

There is a possibility that state legislatures will enact accountability laws
that will further regulate all learning situations. The testing and teaching standards currently set by state legislatures and administered by state boards may
someday add accountability regulations to homeschooling. Currently, there is
a "wave" of educational reforms to improve education. These improvements
include uniform curriculum and uniform student performance within the
curriculum. Such issues of conformity may eventually extend to homeschool
situations (Carper, 2000).

Structure

Religious Organizations

Before 1995, the majority of parents choosing to homeschool did so for religious reasons (Lines, 2000a). From 1970 (when most states enacted compulsory attendance laws) to 1986, when homeschooling was accepted as an alternative to meet attendance regulations in all 50 states, Christian families were
struggling to gain the legislative right to homeschool (Taylor, 1997). These
families formed the first parent support groups, legal support associations,
and lobbies for legislation. Early curriculum materials were developed for or
by these Christian parent organizations. Statutes that allow homeschooling
emerged in many states through the pioneer work and attention of such
Christian parent groups.

Today, curriculum materials are available in all forms, and parents of Jewish, Muslim, and/or other religions can locate support groups as well as materials (Hill, 2000). Parents who choose to homeschool can contact a variety of organizations for support, training, and materials. Organizations that provide materials usually require some type of membership. Such a range of materials necessitates that the parent cautiously evaluate the materials, goals of the organization, ideology of the organization, and the needs of the child.

Educational Institutions

Although homeschool parents are fiercely independent and want to separate the homeschool totally from the formal public school, the effects of educational institutions is difficult (but not entirely impossible) to escape. The influence of educational institutions occurs in several ways. Some parents fear their children could miss the important sequence of instruction and try to follow the curriculum used in the public school. These parents may move their children ahead or spend more time on a concept, but the sequence remains similar. Other parents use materials provided by the school or they buy the same materials used by the school, thereby shaping the homeschool experience (Hill, 2000; Taylor, 1997).

Testing practices of educational institutions can shape the home learning also. Parents who want their children to pass the exit tests at particular grade levels, such as the end of high school, are influenced by test content, just as public school teachers are. While most universities accept homeschooled students without transcripts, students must be successful on the entrance exams. In such cases, college entrance exams shape, for a period of time, the homeschool experience.

Technology

New technology has impacted instruction in public and private schools as well as everyday life. In particular, the use of the Internet to quickly find information on people, things, and places has provided a rich source for parents who are developing curriculum. Additionally, using the Internet provides students with a classroom-style instruction right at home. Parents can purchase online, packaged curriculum that delivers text online, provides recorded lessons, periodic live chats, and a bulletin board/forum to post questions, and administers tests electronically (Farris & Woodruff, 2000).

Satellite television offers another option. Although the format is similar to the traditional lecture, the student can watch the lesson with visual effects and listen to a very high caliber instructor. The instructor delivers the content to persons who can subscribe and connect to the service (Farris & Woodruff, 2000).

Farris and Woodruff (2000) warn parents to be very watchful as students begin to explore the Internet. There are all kinds of sites and information available. A child may advance beyond a parent's imagination and become a cyberspace "internaut" (Hallam, 1994) who knows sites of questionable educational value.

Parents Who Teach at Home

The most influential factor that shapes the homeschool is the parent (Kasperitis, 2000). The parent designs the curriculum and selects as well as provides or secures the resources to begin the student's home learning experience. Decisions on the best use of resources may range from the purchase of traditional books to the purchase of a computer-based instructional program. There are packaged curricula across all the traditional content areas in book and computer formats. With the child's skill levels in mind, the parent may elect to plan and select the materials in concert with the child. After these preliminary decisions, the parent delivers or teaches the curriculum.

Parents can create the environment for learning. In a relaxed, secure setting, children can be encouraged to respond in their individual ways. Parents can nurture a love for lifelong learning about all things as the children engage in daily, real-life home activities. The learning, therefore, occurs in a loving, caring environment created by the parent (Ishizuka, 2000).

The parent plans (again, sometimes with the child) the schedule of classes or learning time. At home, learning does not have to be confined to times that are designated for one subject or another. All time can be learning time. All experiences can be planned learning experiences. The home setting allows for great flexibility.

Supplemental experiences, those in addition to home instruction by the parent, include tutoring in the home or outside the home and special interest activities outside the home. Parents who recognize an academic need that cannot be filled adequately may hire tutors. For example, a parent might seek a tutor for Spanish or for a difficult high school math unit. Parents may hire persons with special talents to provide dance, music, art, martial arts, and/or other special instruction.

Some supplemental opportunities available outside the home for only minimal membership fees provide instruction in small groups, which additionally provide social interaction with other young people. Some of these include Little League baseball, soccer leagues, YMCA/YWCA athletic teams, Girl and Boy scouts, 4-H groups, and public sponsored activities at county and city libraries. State and national parks also provide workshops and one-day camps on wildlife and related topics. Many of the above activities receive support from city or county public funds.

Librarians report an increase in the use of the library by homeschooled children. The librarians comment that, besides a child's free selection of books, parents make special requests related to developing study units based on student interest or linked to a current event. Sometimes parent requests are most difficult because the material was needed yesterday or immediately and some popular materials are checked out quickly. In such cases, pre-planning the study units provide ample time to help secure videos, books, CDs, and other library materials in advance (Masters, 1996). With increased use of the library by homeschoolers, librarians increasingly are grappling with ways to meet the demands for technology, personalized service, and popular subjects that extend beyond the resources of the library. In response to these demands, librarians attempt to address the needs of homeschoolers with interlibrary loan services, extended borrowing time, maintaining homeschooling resource lists, providing public speaker seminars, holding additional story hours, exhibiting at home school conferences, and subscribing to home school journals (Masters, 1996).

Some school districts have designed programs to assist parents with homeschooling (Dahm, 1996; Lines, 2000b). In the more structured situations, the school district can count the homeschoolers in the state attendance reports, which becomes an incentive for public schools to develop part-time options and support services for parents that homeschool. Not all situations, however, allow the public school to count the homeschooled student for attendance. There appears to be a trend for public schools to provide some services and options, which include public school–planned curricula and materials for use at home, online study at home, testing services, and the use of computer labs and software (Lines, 2000b). In one state, if the parent wants specialized assistance, home-study teachers travel to homes to assist parents, (Taylor, 1997). Some states allow homeschooled students to participate on a part-time basis for sports, tournaments (both academic and athletic), and extracurricular activities. In California, the charter school law permits the enrollment of home-schoolers. One California charter is a homeschool organization that provides materials and other support for homeschooling.

Parents have many options that require many decisions, and some require considerable investment. The decision to accept the help of schools and other organization rests with the homeschool designer, the parent, who controls the homeschool and creates a plan that individually fits his/her child. The resources needed to do this may vary, depending on the needs of the child, design or desires of the parent, and resources parents are willing to commit to homeschooling.

Advantages and Disadvantages

Opportunities for Creative Teacher/Tutors

Tutors, to supplement homeschooling and the collaboration with public schools, have created new employment opportunities for teachers, certified and noncertified. Homeschooling parents seek out enriching experiences for their children. Private, specialized instruction often supplements the home academic program for parents who search for enrichment. One example of such a specialized instructional program began when a teacher decided to become a consultant for homeschooling. This teacher offered a unique science program called the Seventh Planet. Students had to devise ways to move a colony through space and establish that colony in a hostile environment. As part of the project, each student had to devise experiments to test the plausibility of the next step toward colonization. Students came to his classroom, and each paid $100 per month. When the local school learned of the project, the teacher was hired as a consultant to provide the same program within the school. While special talents or skills, such as martial arts, music, art, and gymnastics have long been used by homeschooling parents, now some creative teachers in basic content areas are finding a market for innovative teaching (Lines, 2000b).

New teaching positions related to homeschooling have emerged within the public school system. Traveling teachers offer training and guidance to parents in the home, homeschool coordinators help plan part-time school activities, and facilitators manage computer labs and online lessons for homeschoolers. Writing curriculum materials for traditional presentation and online presentation offers still another employment opportunity. Curriculum materials developed by private organizations for homeschooling can be found advertised in a variety of ways, including the Internet and more unconventional means, such as highway billboards. Persons with special teaching and technological skills are creating new options for parents and employment for themselves.

Homeschooling Parents Must Be Prepared

Parents must be prepared for the increased responsibilities on many levels. Ishizuka (2000) advised parents who embark on this adventure to gather information. Handbooks and guides provide assistance to parents who are considering homeschool. Two such guides by Moore and Moore (1996) and Ishizuka (2000) address decision-making issues as well as provide how-to information about schooling. Periodicals as well as educational journals can provide an overview of homeschooling. Parents and children have written autobiographical accounts of homeschooling experiences. Librarians can direct parents to these kinds of sources as well as to doctoral dissertations and masters theses on the subject of homeschooling (Kasperitis, 2000; Schnaiberg, 1996). Many research projects are case studies and read like stories about learning in the home. Such accounts introduce the challenges to parents in a personal way by parents who speak from experience.

Another issue to be considered is having the child at home full time. Ishizuka (2000) reminds parents that there are many things to consider beyond withdrawing the child from the formal school setting. She insists that parents must address issues of tension caused between parents and children with the increased time together, the loss of parental freedom that was provided by the buitd-in, babysitter—the school—the increased demand for time and energy to design and implement lessons as well as search for materials, the shift in family roles when the parent also becomes the teacher, and the need for family backup to help with the children in times of emergency. Family backup may come from the spouse or a relative.

Handbooks (Ishizuka, 2000; Moore & Moore, 1996) alert parents to be prepared for criticism from relatives, local community friends, and other citizens. Some parents prepare an information sheet with recent articles about homeschooling. When the in-laws or neighbors question the legitimacy, legality, and history of becoming the teacher at home, the fact sheet tells the story. Typically, questions are in regard to concern for the child's academic preparation.

The child who will be homeschooled is the primary concern. Ishizuka (2000) suggests that the parent should prepare the child for the new learning arrangements. Children often have to explain the home learning situation to other children or to adults outside the home. Parents can prepare and support children for such questions by talking to the child about homeschooling, the plan, the benefits, the reasons for homeschooling, and the overall nature of the homeschooling experience (2000).

The criticism that educators typically level at homeschooling is the isolation of homeschooled children from other children or groups of children (Medlin, 2000). Critics express concern for the social adjustment of children and suggest that the isolated situation may not support a healthy social and psychological development. Parents must be prepared for such criticism in two ways. First, parents can plan social activities outside the home with a variety of age groups and young people from different social, economic, and racial groups. This provides proof that the children are not isolated and are regulated only to social interaction within the family. Additionally, parents can point to studies that describe homeschooled students, which indicate that those students included in these research studies have many social activities outside the home and that the students appear to be well adjusted socially (Ensign, 1997; Farris & Woodruff, 2000; Medlin, 2000; Ray, 2000).

Some critics accuse homeschooling of deflecting energy and financial support for public schools that are the foundation for a citizenry to support and maintain a democratic society. The federal constitution placed education domain of individual states to establish an educational system that would support the continued common good of a democratic society. Critics say that when public funds are used to enable some groups to leave school, the students left behind suffer from diminished resources, which cripples the public schools to properly respond and prepare all for a democratic society. This leads to more stratification and fragmentation of society (Apple, 2000; Kohn, 1998; Lubienski, 2000). To address this criticism, parents can involve children in community projects that show concern for all levels within society, that recognize and address social injustices, and that recognize and address economic injustices.

Summary

When a parent considers homeschooling, the decision is much more complex than simply withdrawing a child from a school, public or private. Parents immediately become more involved with increased requirements of time and re-sources. Parents step out of the bureaucracy of public and private schools into what they hope would be a secure home setting that is flexible, caring, and in-dividualized. Both, the parent and the children, determine curriculum con-tent that at times may or may not include spiritual development, and in the relaxed home setting parent and child participate in learning experiences. The parent, the decision maker, and the designer for a homeschooling setting has the opportunity and the responsibility.

Resources

The following list of organizations and materials that follow are not endorsed by the authors, but are offered as examples of resources that are available. A search of the Internet calls to the screen over 1,000 suggestions. Parents are advised and cautioned to examine carefully all materials and sources. Authors and agencies do not list affiliations, which at times can only be learned by di-rectly questioning the publisher or source.

Curriculum Materials

Home School Curriculum Kit
800-622-3070
http://www.homeschooling.com

Critical Thinking Books & Software*
P.O. Box 448
Pacific Grove CA 93950
800-458-4849
http://www.criticalthinking.com
*Books, tapes, and CDs grouped by grades . . . 2—4, 2–7, 7–12 etc.; prices range $18.95–$23.95 for sets.

The Sycamore Tree
2179 Meyers Place
Costa Mesa CA 92627
800-779-6750
http://www.sycamoretree.com

Bob Jones University Press
800-845-5731
Well-known and widely used materials with Christian beliefs incorporated
within the lessons.

Smarterville.com
Kids' software that gives you more! (Reading and Math)

The Clavert School*
105 Tuscany Road
Baltimore, MD 21210
410-243-6030
*Offers CD-ROMs, videos (all curriculum to plan a home school program)

Oregon Institute of Science and Medicine*
2251 Dick George Road
Cave Junction, OR 97523
*Curriculum for grades 1–12; complete courses on computer, plus they are
"Saxon" book representatives.

Keystone National
420 West 5th Street
Bloomsburg, PA 17815
800-255-4937
http://www.keystonehighschool.com

Newsletters

Christian Brotherhood
229 School Street
Azle, TX 76020
800-527-9501

Video Courses

A Beka Book, Inc.
P.O. Box 19100
Pensacola, FL 32523
800-874-2352
http://www.abeka.com

CD-ROM

Play 'N Talk*
7105 Manzanita Street
Carlsbad, CA 92009
619-438-4330
*Programs range from $250–$379

Organizations

Texas Home School Coalition
P.O. Box 6982
Lubbock, TX 79493
http://www.thsc.org

Home School Legal Defense Assoc.
P.O. Box 3000
Purcellville, VA 20134

SETHA (Southeast Texas Homeschool Association)
4950 FM 1960 W. Ste. C3-87
Houston, TX 77069

Books

Common Sense Press
904-475-5757

Christian Liberty
800-443-7323
http://www.homeschool.net

Sonlight Curriculum
303-730-6292
http://www.sonlight.com

Alpha Omega
800-622-3070
http://www.home-schooling.com

Rod & Staff
606-522-4348

The Classics
800-460-7171
http://www.classichome.com

Quality Children's
800-344-3198

Greenleaf Press
800-311-1508
http://www.greenleafpress.com

Saxon
800-225-5750
http://www.saxonpub.com

EPS
800-558-9595
http://www.epsbooks.com

Masco Science
800-558-9595
http://www.ensco.com

Internet Resources

- *http://www.homeschoolfun.com/assoc.html*
  This site has over 27 printed pages referring to support groups from all 50 states.

- Jon's Homeschool Resource Page
  This is perhaps the largest collection of homeschool resources.
  http://www.midnightbeach.com

- UK home resources page—UK resources
  http://www.ici.uk/evansjon/home.html

- Kids Connect is a question-and-answer help and referral service for K–12 students on the Internet. Students use e-mail to contact and receive a response within two days from a volunteer library media specialist. *AskKC@als.org*

- Ask Dr. Math is a service for elementary, middle, and high school students and is administered by students and professors at Swarthmore College in Swarthmore, PA. *dr.math@forum.swarthmore.edu.*

- USENET newsgroups are on an electronic bulletin board system on thousands of topics. These bulletin boards provide a way for parents who are teaching at home to chat with other teachers or persons interested in a topic. Some examples are: k12.ed.art- (on arts and crafts for K–12 grades. Users should contact their system operator for instructions for Usenet Newsgroups.

Additional Resources

Bell, D. (2001). *The ultimate guide to homeschooling.* Year 2001 edition. Palmyra, PA: Debra Bell's Home School Resource Center.

Colfax, D., & Colfax, M. (1988). *Homeschooling for excellence.* New York: Warner Books.

Dobson, L. (2000). *Homeschoolers' success stories: 15 adults and 12 young people share the impact that homeschooling has made on their lives.* Roseville, CA; Prima Publishing.

Griffith, M. (1999). *The homeschooling handbook: From preschool to high school, a parent's guide.* Revised 2nd edition. Roseville, CA: Prima Publishing.

Guterson, D. (1992). *Family matters: Why homeschooling makes sense.* New York: Harcourt, Brace & Jovanovich.

Hendrickson, B. (1994). *Homeschool: Taking the first step.* Mountain Meadow Press.

Rupp, R. (1999). *Getting started on home learning: How and why to teach your kids at home.* New York: Three Rivers Press.

Annual Home School Conferences

Arlington, Texas (May)

Gulf Coast Home School Conference (sponsored by SETHA) Houston, Texas (May)

Chapter References

Aizenman, N. C. (October 19, 2000). Blacks in Prince George's join home-schooling trend. *Washington Post.* [Online]. Available: *http://www.washingtonpost.com /wp-dynarticles /A36262-200Oct18.html.*

Alexander, K. & Alexander, M. D. (2001). *American public school law.* New York: West Publishing.

American Association of School Administrators (April 17, 2000). Kansas district finds way to bring home-schooled students back into the public education fold. *Leadership News AASA.* [Online]. Available: *http://www.aasa.org/In/Misc/-4-17-00vcs.htm.*

Apple, M. W. (2000). The cultural politics of home schooling. *Peabody Journal of Education,* 75 (1 & 2), 256–271.

Arai, A. B. (September 6, 1999). Homeschooling and the redefinition of citizenship. *Education Policy Analysis Archives,* 7(27). [Online]. Available: *http://www.epaa.asu .edu/epaa/v7n27.html.*

Blair, J. (March 29, 2000). New college set to welcome home-schooled students in the fall. *Education Week,* 19 (29), 5.

Carper, J. C. (2000). Pluralism to establishment to dissent: The religious and educational context of home schooling. *Peabody Journal of Education,* 75 (1 & 2), 8–19.

Crowson, R. L. (2000). The home schooling movement: A few concluding observations. *Peabody Journal of Education,* 75 (1 & 2), 294–300.

Dahm, L. (1996). Education at home, with help from school. *Educational Leadership,* 54(2), 68–71.

Ensign, J. (2000). Defying the stereotypes of special education: Home school students. *Peabody Journal of Education*, 75 (1 & 2), 147–158.

Farris, M. P., & Woodruff, S. A. (2000). The future of home schooling. *Peabody Journal of Education.* 75 (1 & 2), 233–256.

Hallam, S. (October 14, 1994) Ground rules for all cyberspace internauts. *The Times Higher Education Supplement,* no. 1145.

Hill, P. T. (2000). Home schooling and the future of public education. *Peabody Journal of Education*, 75 (1 & 2), 20–31.

Ishizuka, K. (2000). *The unofficial guide to homeschooling.* New York: IDG Books Worldwide.

Kasperitis, B. (2000). *Multiple case studies of home schooling: Looking for emerging patterns.* Masters thesis from Stephen F. Austin State University, Nacogdoches, Texas.

Kleiner, C. (October 16, 2000). Home school come of age. *U.S. News,* 129, (15) 54.

Kohn, A. (1998). Only for my kid. *Phi Delta Kappan,* 79 (8), 568–577.

Lines, P.M. (2000a). Homeschooling comes of age. *Educational Leadership,* 54 (2) 63–67.

Lines, P. M. (2000b). When home schoolers go to school: A partnership between families and schools. *Peabody Journal of Education,* 75 (1 & 2), 159–186.

Lubienski, C. (2000). Whither the common good? A critique of home schooling. *Peabody Journal of Education,* 75 (1 & 2), 207–232.

McDowell, S. A. (2000). Toward a theory of social integration. *Peabody Journal of Education,* 75 (1 & 2), 187–206.

McDowell, S. A., & Ray, B. D. (2000). The home education movement in context, practice, and theory. *Peabody Journal of Education,* 75 (1 & 2), 1–7.

McDowell, S. A., Sanchez, A. R., & Jones, S. S. (2000). Participation and perception: Looking at home schooling through a multicultural lens. *Peabody Journal of Education,* 75 (1 & 2), 124–146.

Masters, D. G. (1996). Public library services for home schooling. ERIC Clearinghouse. Reproduction ED402936.

Medlin, R. G. (2000). Home schooling and the question of socialization. *Peabody Journal of Education,* 75 (1 & 2), 107–123.

Moore, R., & Moore, D. (1996). A successful homeschool handbook. Nashville, TN: Thomas Nelson Publishers.

Ray, B. D. (2000). Home schooling. The ameliorator of negative influences on learning. *Peabody Journal of Education,* 75 (1 & 2), 71–106.

Rudner, L. M. (1998). Scholastic achievement and demographic characteristics of home school students in 1998. *Education Policy Analysis Archives,* 7 (8). [Online]. Available: *http://www.Epaa.asu.edu/epaa/v7/n8.*

Schnaiberg, L. (June 12, 1996). Staying home from school. *Education Week.* [Online]. Available: *http://www.edweed.org/we/vol-15/38home.h15.*

Sherwood, T. (1989). *Nontraditional education in rural districts.* ERIC Reproduction Number ED308054.

Taylor, L. A. (1996). Home in school: Insights on education through the lens of home schoolers. *Theory into Practice,* 36 (2), 110–116.

Welner, K. M., & Welner, K. G. (1999). Contextualizing the homeschooling data: A response to Rudner. Education Policy Analysis Archives, 7 (13). [Online]. Available: *http://www.Epaa.asu.edu/epaa/v7/n13.html.*

Choosing Wisely for Our Children

Sandra Harris, Ph.D.

". . . Unless you project hope for [children], your efforts to teach
them to read, write, and calculate won't make a profound difference."
Herb Kohl (cited in Scherer, 1998, p. 9).

There is no doubt that education reform has become a priority for each of our 50 states ("Honoring the Past by Preparing for the Future," 2000). In fact, each state is involved in some form of rigorous examination and monitoring of student performance to improve educational levels of our children in public schools. Results of these high stakes tests are reported to the public, and drop-out rates and graduation rates are closely monitored (Brown, 1999). Additionally, other ways to bring about change within the education community are also considered that focus on the structure of the school, the school culture, leadership, and on the teachers, themselves (Harris, 2000). Despite good intentions, however, too often the most overlooked in education are the children themselves.

Therefore, the challenge to parents and educators is to consistently focus all efforts on what is best for the child. This can happen best when educators and parents work together to build a learning community that extends beyond support of local schools to that of support of children and the individual learning needs they have. This ethic of care is relational and is primarily concerned with how people treat one another. In fact, in the complex times of the 21st century, we are reminded that the "need for care in our present culture is acute" (Noddings, 1992, p. xi). Thus, as parents and as educators, we are challenged to consider *with care* the needs of our children and then to choose wisely which school setting would be the one that offers each child the greatest opportunity to succeed. As educators, we must also consider which school setting offers the greatest opportunity for teachers and faculty to work successfully with children. Clearly, school choice is a necessary reform structure for children, as well as for educators. Without it, the best choice to meet a child's needs might not be available, or beyond the resources of caring parents and educators. We offer hope to children when we have choices; we offer more hope when we choose wisely.

Chapter Resources

Brown, R. (1999). Creating school accountability reports. *The School Administrator,* 19 (56), 12–17.

Harris, S. (2000). Creating a climate for school reform that will last: Five critical factors. *Catalyst for Change,* 30 (1), 11–13.

Honoring the past by preparing for the future. (2000). *Phi Delta Kappan,* 81 (5), 338.

Noddings, N. (1992). *The challenge to care in schools: An alternative approach to education.* New York: Teachers College Press.

Scherer, M. (1998). Discipline of hope: A conversation with Herb Kohl. *Educational Leadership,* 56 (1), 8–13.

Chapter Ten

What to Look for in Good Schools

Patrick M. Jenlink, Ed.D.

The strength of a democratic society lies in a well-educated and authentically engaged citizenry. However, strength alone is not sufficient for a democratic society to flourish. The success of a democratic society lies equally in its capacity for social justice, equity, and caring and to manifest these values in its citizenry. The key to a strong and successful democracy is its educational system (Dewey, 1916), for it is here that every citizen grows into her/his understanding of the ideal of democraty in America. This ideal of democracy is one founded on the principles of freedom, liberty, and the right of choice in the conduct of matters concerning one's government. It is, most importantly, in the combination of these basic principles, with choice as a culminating factor, that gives vitality to and ensures opportunity for a democratic way of life.

Choice, ever present in the day-to-day lives of individuals, has permeated the fabric of the American way of life, becoming manifest in the organizations, communities, schools, and families of our society. Importantly, the prominence of choice in America has gained new currency in recent years as parents and citizens, from the large urban cities, suburban communities, and small rural towns, have turned their attention critically to the issues of our educational system and the disparities that exist in the quality of schools. Access to quality education for all children stands at the forefront of these issues, as does an increasing concern for our children's safety and well-being.

Nearly a century ago, John Dewey (1902) said, "What the best and wisest parent wants for his own child, that must the community want for all its children. Any other ideal for our schools is narrow and unlovely; acted upon, it destroys our democracy" (p. 3). School choice, as a movement in America (and around the world), has rekindled the words of Dewey once more, bringing to the foreground of public discourse the rights and responsibilities of parents in the educational decisions of their children. Elmore and Fuller (1996) reflect in their analysis of parent involvement and school choice that "virtually everyone in our democratic society—increasingly skeptical of institutional authority—agrees that parents should exercise some control over their educational choices" (p. 188). However, with control over educational choices comes social responsibility. Dewey (1973, 1981), in his vision of the school in a democratic society, considered the school as a social and transformative institution for redressing many of the inequities emergent in American society. It was, Dewey believed, through the education of children that "society [could] formulate for its own purposes [and] organize its own means and resources" (p. 443).

The increasing momentum of the choice movement brings new meaning to Dewey's notion of a society formulating its own purposes, specifically as parents seek to provide the best for their children. This is most evident as parents experience community schools faced with increasing difficulty in providing the quality of education expected for their children, as well as equal access to quality of education that most parents want for their children, but many are denied. Perhaps even more significant in parents' increased interest in school choice is the realization that many schools are not safe, caring environments for children. As Sernak (1998) notes, we live in "a world fraught with violence, anguish, hatred, and disregard for life, where learning how to care for one another is critical to our survival" (p. 146). Noddings (1992), in speaking to the importance of caring in schools, admonishes us that "the need for care in our present culture is acute" (p. xi). The choice of parents for a school is often heavily weighted by the concern for not only for a "good school" in terms of academic quality, but a "good school" that offers the protective dimensions of caring.

Caring Schools for Children

In the best of all worlds, where child poverty did not exist, where racial and ethnic inequities did not exist, where youth violence did not exist, where social injustices did not permeate the lives of our children, and where an ethic of care was the standard for all humanity, we would find the security, prosperity, and ideals of America safe from any external or internal enemy. In the best of all worlds, our children would leave home each day and go to a school characterized as caring, just, and equitable. Unfortunately, we do not live in the best of all worlds, and when our children leave home for school, they are not always afforded a caring, just, and equitable place for learning.

The need for choice in selecting schools is more evident than ever, as is the need for using an ethic of care in making choices, particularly in the decisions that manifest in parents selecting a school for their child. Outside of the family, schools are the primary arenas for promoting caring, a value and ethic that have strong currency in everyday life (Chaskin & Rauner, 1995). An ethic of care serves to guide wise decisions in selecting caring schools for our children. Caring schools are characterized both by a type of relationship, ethical in nature, as well as a capacity of individuals and collectives to care for the self and for others (Noddings, 1992, 1993). Schools where an ethic of care is present embody the tenets of *connection, particularity of responsibilities, reciprocity, and commitment* (Sernak, 1998).

Connection implies that a web or circle of relationships (Noddings, 1984) is at the core of the school's work with children, parents, and community. It signifies the development of interdependence rather than independence. *Particularity of responsibilities* suggests that "ubiquitous rules and principles do not apply, for caring is based in the specific context" (Sernak, 1998, p. 11) of the school, and therefore is not universal to all schools. Responsibilities and relationships of all individuals (students, teachers, parents, administrators, etc.) are at its center, rather than rights and rules. *Reciprocity* is necessary to completing and sustaining caring relationships. In the caring school, both caregivers and care receivers—teachers and students, teachers and parents, parents and students—are evident (Sernak, 1998). The needs of the child (student) are always at the forefront of activity, guiding the ethical considerations and academic decisions. *Commitment,* perhaps the most important, implies a type of bond, loyalty, and "joint 'knowing' or awareness of caring between people" (Sernak, 1998, p. 12).

The caring school exemplifies a concern with "how human beings meet and treat one another. It is not unconcerned with individual rights, the common good, or community traditions, but it de-emphasizes these concepts and recasts them in terms of relation" (Noddings, 1993, p. 45).

Caring schools also exemplify caring as a value and a moral imperative that moves "self-determination into social responsibility and uses knowledge and strategic thinking to decide how to act in the best interests of others. Caring binds individuals to their society, to their communities, and to each other" (Webb, Wilson, Corbett, & Mordecai, 1993, p. 33–34). In caring schools, a concern for and commitment to being culturally responsive to the diverse needs of all students is evident.

Choice as Social Responsibility

Education is not just preparation for economic life and citizenship. It is, as Dewey (1902) insisted, life itself. Dewey wanted an education for every child that would match that child's interests and capacities. Choice of schools is about the social responsibility of parents to choose the school that affords a just and equitable education. Choice is also about the citizenry giving voice to the needs of a diverse population of students, providing the best of all opportunities for life by having the best of all opportunities through education. Social responsibility through exercising choice in schools ameliorates the disparities found in quality of schools and quality of learning experiences that children have in schools.

Choice in the schools that children attend is choice in life itself. Parents must be actively engaged in making decisions (choices) that guide the education of their child on one level, and of all children in the community, on another level of social responsibility. Choice—as liberty—seeks fair or just distribution of society's goods (Noddings, 1999). Choice also seeks equity in treatment of society's members—in particular, of society's children.

Expanding the Scope of Choice in Schools

Making the right choices for children is, for parents, perhaps the greatest challenge and certainly the most important of responsibilities they face on a daily basis. Nowhere is this more evident than in choosing a child's education. Historically, Americans have always had "choice" based on where they take up residence. The attendance-zone model of school choice (Godwin, Kemerer, Martinez, & Ruderman, 1998) is recognized as a minimal option, and the most often used in choosing a school. Unfortunately, not all geographical areas are aligned with the quality of schools parents want for their child. More problematic has been the issue of "access to educational opportunity" for children of minority families, low socioeconomic families, and other marginalized families. Choice has more often been afforded to those individuals of wealth and means who could purchase options, either with fiscal, political, or cultural currency, thus giving way to a growing inequity in the education of America's children.

Choice, as we are seeing it redefined today, has the potential for increasing options for all children, even within the neighborhood community. As the choice movement has grown and the scope of the options available to all citizens has expanded, "many families are likely to gain opportunities now limited only to the wealthy, and hence the assumption that parents are the agents best able to make educational decisions on the part of their children would have greater impact on social outcomes . . . than in the case of the current educational system" (Gintis, 1995, p. 498).

Choice also has the potential for increasing the options for teachers and other professionals who have historically been limited to either the public school system or private or parochial schools. With the advent of choice schools, the spectrum of professional opportunities has widened, and educators may now exercise a type of choice in selecting a school. Importantly, the tensions created by the school choice movement stimulates innovative changes in educational settings, providing for improved programs and academic experiences, both for students and for educators.

The scope of options for choice in schools has enlarged significantly since the 1950s when choice first entered the educational and political arenas (Elmore & Fuller, 1996). However, the judicial arena had already set the tone in America for choice at the turn of the 20th century with precedents by the Supreme Court in *Pierce v. Society of Sisters* (1925), where parents' rights to choose private schools and direct the education of their children were recognized. Over the decades, constitutional and legal challenges prompted by parental actions continued to lay the groundwork school choice. *Brown v. Board of Education* (1954), perhaps one of the most significant landmark cases, forever changed education when access to equal educational opportunity was affirmed for African-American students.

Following is a comprehensive although not definitive set of options available to parents (based on state and/or local policy). The options build on the heritage of parental struggles in the courts, the political arenas, and the schoolhouse to provide not only equality of opportunity but to provide equity and justice as well as academic quality for all children.

Attendance-zone schools. Traditional neighborhood or community-based public schools supported by the state education system. Schools are aligned with residential location and bureaucratically determined catchment zones. Choice of school is determined by taking up residence (Godwin, Kemerer,

Martinez, & Ruderman, 1998; Schneider, Teske, & Marschall, 2000; Unger, 1999a).

Intradistrict-choice. Allows children to choose and attend any public school within the school district where they live—but nowhere else—at public expense, including costs of transportation to and from school, textbooks and other school materials. Depending on the specific plan, the range of choice may include a few to all schools in a district (Cookson, 1994; Unger, 1999a).

Interdistrict-choice. Allows children to attend any public school in or outside their home district—crossing district lines—within state limits, although not necessarily at public expense. Tuition funds from the state follow the student, and transportation costs are usually provided (Cookson, 1994; Unger, 1999a).

Extrasystem choice. Allows children to transfer outside the public school system in which they live, to a private or parochial school. Typically, the parents are issued vouchers or the equivalency, with a dollar value equal to the tax dollars that would have been spent on their child's education (including transportation) in the district in which the children live (Unger, 1999a).

Controlled-choice. A program that requires parents to choose a school within a community, with choices controlled or restricted to ensure the racial, gender, and socioeconomic balance of each school. Such programs may reflect a strategy to comply with court-ordered desegregation, or may provide opportunity for voluntary desegregation and/or promote parental choice of schools as a major goal of district-wide reform. Controlled-choice plans differ from other choice plans (such as open-enrollment and voucher models) by not relying on market competition among schools to generate school improvement. Controlled choice can also be implemented as an intradistrict plan, in which several zones or subdistricts are created that can include magnet programs (Cookson, 1994; Coons & Sugarman, 1999; Peterkin & Jackson, 1994).

Magnet schools. Public schools that offer specialized programs, often intentionally designed and located to attract students to otherwise unpopular areas or schools. Magnet schools were originally created to promote racial balance but have since evolved to include innovative opportunities, increase educational choices and improve standards (Black, 1996; Douzenis, 1994; Goldring & Smrekar, 2000; Farmer & Farmer, 2000).

Homeschooling. An education program that is parent (or guardian) directed outside the public school and inside the student's home. Parents provide the educational programs, based on state requirements, and with consideration for the needs of the child. Decisions to home school are often related to disagreements with academic and ideological reasons as well as based on religious beliefs (Martin, 1991; Ray, 2000; Russo & Gordon, 1996; Unger, 1999a).

Private/parochial schools. Elementary or secondary schools controlled by other than a state or subdivision of a state, or the federal government. Schools may be church supported/sponsored, military, or otherwise independent from the public school system. The schools are usually supported by other than public funds and the operation of programs is the responsibility of other than publicly elected or appointed officials (Anderson & Resnick, 1997; Center for Education Statistics, 1987; Cookson, 1991).

Postsecondary options. Programs that enable high school students to enroll in college courses, often times while concurrently enrolled in the public school, and paid for through public support. The courses students take often contribute to high school graduation requirements as well as to their college programs (Cookson,1994; Coons & Sugarman, 1999).

Second-chance programs. Alternative schools and programs for students who have difficulties in standard public school settings. Two broad categories define these programs. The first includes programs for students who have either dropped out of school, are pregnant or are parents, have been assessed as chemically dependent, or have been expelled from their previous school. A second category includes programs that are more clearly aligned with academic needs of students otherwise disenchanted by the traditional offerings of the public school or students whose academic needs exceed the available offerings of the public school (Cookson,1994; Coons & Sugarman, 1999; Raywid, 1998).

Charter schools. Publicly sponsored autonomous schools that are substantially free of direct administrative control by state government but are held accountable for achieving certain levels of student performance (and other specified outcomes). These schools are often designed around a special theme and through parental and community involvement to provide alternative educational opportunities for students. Charter schools may be sponsored or chartered by partner universities or other educational entities within the state. The charter of such a school stipulates academic, organizational, and financial standards for which the school will be held accountable by the sponsoring or chartering entity (Coons & Sugarman, 1999; Jenkins & Dow, 1996; Nathan, 1996; Viteritti, 1999).

Workplace training. Programs that provide apprenticeship opportunities for students to learn a skilled trade not offered through existing vocational training. Typically, costs are divided between the employer and the school district. These programs may be intradistrict or interdistrict in nature (Cookson, 1994).

Voucher plan. A system or program based on the award of certificate or cash payments by the state that enables public school students to attend schools of their choice, public or private, interdistrict or extrasystem. Vouchers have a fixed value based on the tuition costs within the district where the student lives and generally includes transportation costs. Vouchers are redeemed at the time of enrollment (Chubb & Moe, 1990; Cookson, 1994; Coons & Sugarman, 1999; Martin, 1991; Moe, 1995).

Tuition tax credits. A system of funding choice that allows parents to receive credit against their income tax (state and/or local) if their child attends a nonpublic (private or parochial) school (Cookson, 1994; Coons & Sugarman, 1999; Harris, Ford, Wilson, & Sandidge, 1991).

EMO programs. Educational Management Organizations (EMOs) are for-profit management companies that contract with public and private (intradistrict and interdistrict) schools to provide educational management programs. Such programs are exempt under contract from many of the state and/or local policy constraints on public schools. Many of the EMOs have curriculum and instruction systems as well as classroom management programs that are implemented in the contracted school (Cazares, 1997; Doughty, 1997; Edwards, 1997; Hill, Pierce, & Guthrie, 1997).

The range of options has increased within and across our educational system, although the availability of all options varies based on state and local policy (within and across each state). The ability of some students to attend private/parochial schools (or schools that are non-public supported) may remain limited based on socioeconomic status. Importantly, by judicial actions and political and policy decisions, there has been considerable effort to eliminate the marginalization of families based on race, ethnicity, gender, and other factors that characterize earlier discrimination and segregation.

Choosing Good Schools

The first, and perhaps most difficult question that a parent will ask when trying to choose a school is, "What is a good school?", which is often followed by, "How do I know it is good?" Lightfoot (1983) suggests that the good school is only good in its own context or setting (community, neighborhood, district, etc.). Or, in other words, goodness is not universal to all schools. Goodness is a much more complicated notion that refers to what is often called the ethos or culture of the school, rather than discrete elements. It refers to what makes the school whole, which includes "people, structures, relationships, ideology, goals, intellectual substance, motivation, and will" (Lightfoot, 1983, p. 23). Goodness is a quality that refers to the complex whole.

Choice schools, by design, are diverse in their offerings and, therefore, provide different opportunities to different students. "Good schools" are found across the full range of choice options, but not all choice schools are good, just like not all public schools are good. The reflection of democratic ideals, ethical and moral imperatives of social justice, equity, and caring, as well as academic quality are central to defining a "good school." But the overriding factor in determining the quality of any school is whether or not there is a "goodness of fit" between the needs of the child and programs and culture of the school. This means that parents must ascertain what it is, as Dewey (1902) noted, that they want for their child, guided by the wisdom and concern for the best educational opportunity.

An analysis of research on characteristics of schools (choice and public) that reflect high quality, goodness, and success (Anderson & Resnick, 1997; Godwin, Kemerer, Martinez, & Ruderman, 1998; Harris, Ford, Wilson, & Sandidge, 1991; Jenkins & Dow, 1996; Lightfoot, 1983; Noddings, 1993, 1999; Raywid, 1998; Unger, 1999a, 1999b) suggests that the following points might serve as a heuristic in making choices about the "goodness of fit" of a choice school and the child (student):

- There is an unswerving attitude of care, respect, and trust toward students and parents, which recognizes the place of parental involvement in decisions related to the child's learning.

- There is evidence of provision for safe and regulated environments—youth violence and the threat to a safe and secure setting is monitored and managed.

- There is a public information system that informs parents about the school and provides ease of access to the school for purposes of acquiring information about the school—ease of access includes supportive mechanisms for parents who may or may not have similar educational, cultural, or financial grounds from which to make decisions.

- Beyond an explicit disciplinary code, there is a solid foundation of authority—a symmetry in power and use of power to create the means of coordination of action—and the necessary relationships and discourses required to sustain a coherent organization.

- There are clearly stated academic goals and a clearly defined core curriculum that are culturally responsive to the full range of students representative in a culturally diverse society, community, and school district.

- There is a well-articulated plan for identifying, in concert with the parents, the needs of the student as well as an ongoing strategy for assessing the "goodness of fit" between the school and the needs of the student.

- There are high expectations and academic standards for students, with students expected to adjust upward to high standards rather than standards ever being lowered to adjust to unwilling students.

- There is an emphasis on developing the child's civic responsibilities in a culturally diverse society—recognizing that civic and social responsibilities must be responsive to a changing culture.

- There are high quality teachers who are academically qualified and who create a pleasant, safe, and professional work environment, where highly paid principals and teachers control academic planning.

- There is strong administrative leadership that values the participation of students, teachers, parents, and community members in setting the vision and direction of the school, and works to insure the translation of the vision into every dimension of school and community.

- Symmetry in power relationships exist within the school—between teacher and administrator, teacher and parent, teacher and teacher—and between the school, the parent and the community.

- Extensive opportunity for and balance between high quality academic programs, extracurricular activities, extensive student participation in student government, and community programs are available.

- Strong ethical and moral imperatives guide the decisions with justice, equity, and caring.

- There is financial solvency, with current and future fiscal planning and management strategies that ensure minimal risk to the operations of the school and the continuation of quality programs for all children.

- All activities of the school exemplify the basic tenets of equality of educational opportunity, social tolerance of diversity, social justice, and democracy.

- There is a valuing of strong community and parental support—involvement in decisions related to academics, policy, ideology, and/or other dimensions of the school.

Again, not all schools, whether public or choice, are good, and not all schools will demonstrate all the characteristics identified above. "Goodness" of a school is not a universal principle. Parents must look for those characteristics that meet the criteria they have set for their child and her/his schooling and education. It is important to note that even when a majority of the characteristics are present in a choice school, they must be understood within the unique setting of that school and the reality of its day-to-to operations.

Choosing Wisely

The common feature of all choice programs—whether public or private, intradistrict or interdistrict—is that they are designed to increase the range of educational opportunities available to students outside the boundaries and barriers of the public education systems normally found in the communities where they live (Viteritti, 1999). Wise decisions about which school a parent selects for her/his child are decisions based on information. While the "goodness" of a school is a critical determinant in selecting a school, choice is first and foremost about making an informed decision. Choice is the responsibility of the parent, and should be supported through a clear plan or strategy for gaining information about the school(s) under consideration.

There are a number of sources that a parent can access to build a sufficient information base from which to make an informed decision. Primary in any information gathering is to visit the school(s) under consideration and ask for public information concerning the school. Once the information has been reviewed, the parent should make a list of questions to ask officials at the school, to ask parents of students who currently attend the school, and to use as a guide to access available information via internet services on a computer or to guide library searches at the community or area library.

An informed decision for parents and educators is one that has the fullest spectrum of information behind it, before it is made. This should include but not be limited to such topics (and related sources of information) as:

Academic success of the school	Student achievement results, teacher/administrator interview, parent interview, Internet site, published information
Financial stability of the school	Fiscal reports, teacher/administrator interview, parent interview, publicly recorded budget/accounting reports
Parental involvement in the school	School policy and procedures, parent organizations [PTO, PTA], teacher/administrator interview
Philosophy, mission, goals, vision of the school	School policy, published documents, teacher/administrator interview, parent interview, Internet sites, sponsoring/chartering organization
Admission/selection criteria	School policy, published documents, Internet sites, teacher/administrator interview, parent interview
Professional opportunities for teacher learning and development	School policy and procedure, published information, teacher/administrator interview, parent interview, PTO/PTA
Parental satisfaction	Parent interview, PTO/PTA, teacher/administrator interview, published information
Academic preparation of teachers	Teacher/administrator interview, PTO/PTA, parent interview, school policy/procedure, published information, local/state/national accrediting agency
Leadership quality of school	Teacher interview, parent interview, PTO/PTA, administrator interview

Standards and expectations of	School policy/procedures, parent inter-
school for students/	view, PTO/PTA, teacher/administrator
teachers/programs	interview, published information, Internet
	sites, local/state/national accrediting
	agency).

In preparation for gathering information to guide decisions concerning choice, a set of pragmatic guidelines that might be helpful include:

- Know the needs of the child and the specific preferences about education and schooling,

- Know the sources of information necessary to making an informed decision and the case of access to these sources,

- Know the protocols for contacting individuals, schools, community/state/national organizations related to information gathering,

- Have a plan for collecting, recording, organizing information about the schools (personal contact, phone contact, Internet contact, community or state/national-based organizations [library, accrediting entity, parent or professional organizations, etc.]),

- Allocate sufficient time for information gathering—your time and the time of others who you will need to assist you in the process,

- Organize information for each school and identify strengths/weaknesses, advantages/disadvantages in relation to preferences for schooling and education, and

- Choose the school that has clearest "goodness of fit" for the child's needs and preferences listed.

The school choice options selected for consideration will no doubt present some challenges in terms of collecting information. The uniqueness of each choice option will bring with it a uniqueness in where and how information may be collected, as well as in who will be able to provide information and when it may be collected.

While the pragmatic guidelines help to organize a "rational" approach to studying choice among the different options, it is important to remember that each choice option is unique and context dependent. Equally important to remember is that the nature of the information gathering and choice process is conditioned by the scope and complexity of the options selected for consideration.

Summary

Choice is a basic democratic ideal that permeates the very fabric of American society. The growing presence of choice in matters of schooling and education began with Supreme Court decisions like *Pierce v. Society of Sisters* (1925) and *Brown v. Board of Education* (1954), followed in the 1950s with an emergence of choice as a movement across America that has challenged the very foundations of our public education system. The escalation of "choice" in schools comes at a time when the tremendous diversity of needs that children have today directs our attention to consider the choice option as naturally occurring in response to a growing pluralism in our democratic way of life.

Choosing wisely the education of our children, as Dewey (1902) reminds us, is at the heart of our democracy. Choice of the schools that our children attend is an ethical and social responsibility that carries with it the need to understand what makes a "good" school. It carries with it an ethical and moral imperative to understand what makes a "caring" school and what makes a school a socially just and equitable place for all children, the weakest as well as the strongest.

Choice is about being American. Being American is about advanced citizenship. The responsibility of choice is explicit, the need for choice is apparent, and the path to choice is accessed through an informed and disciplined understanding of the options available and the information necessary for choosing wisely the school and education of each child.

Chapter References

Anderson, K. M., & Resnick, M. A. (1997). *Careful comparisons: Public and private schools in America.* Alexandria, Virginia: National School Boards Association.

Black, S. (1996). The pull of magnets. *The American School Board Journal,* 183 (9), 34–36.

Brown v. Board of Education, 347 U.S. 483 (1954).

Cazares, P. (1997, March). *The private management of public schools: The Hartford, Connecticut experience.* Paper presented at the annual meeting of the American Educational Research Association, Chicago.

Center for Education Statistics (1987). *The condition of education—A statistical report.* Washington, DC: U.S. Department of Education.

Chaskin, R. J., & Rauner, D. M. (1995). Youth and caring. *Phi Delta Kappan,* 76 (9), 667–674.

Chubb, J. E., & Moe, T. M. (1990). *Politics, markets and America's schools.* Washington, DC: Brookings Institution.

Cookson, Jr., P. W., (1991). Private schooling and equity: Dilemmas of choice. *Education and Urban Society,* 23 (2), 185–199.

Cookson, Jr., P. W. (1994). *School choice: The struggle for the soul of American education.* New Haven: Yale University Press.

Coons, J. E., & Sugarman, S. D. (1999). *Education by choice: The case for family control.* Troy, NY: Educator's International Press.

Dewey, J. (1902). *The school and society.* Chicago: University of Chicago Press.

Dewey, J. (1916). *Democracy and education: An introduction to the philosophy of education.* New York: The Free Press.

Dewey, J. (1973, 1981). *The philosophy of John Dewey* (ed. by John J. McDermott). Chicago: University of Chicago Press.

Doughty, S. (1997, March). *The private management of public schools: The Baltimore, Maryland experience.* Paper presented at the annual meeting of the American Educational Research Association, Chicago.

Douzenis, C. (1994). Evaluation of magnet schools: Methodological issues and concerns. *The Clearinghouse,* 15 (18), 494–446.

Edwards, D. L. (1997, March). *The private management of public schools: The Dade County, Florida experience.* Paper presented at the annual meeting of the American Educational Research Association, Chicago.

Elmore, R. F., & Fuller, B. (1996). Empirical research on educational choice: What are the implications for policy-makers? In B. Fuller & R. F. Elmore (Eds.), *Who chooses? who loses? Culture, institutions, and the unequal effects of school choice* (pp. 187–201). New York: Teachers College Press.

Farmer, B. W., & Farmer, E. I. (2000). Organizational structures of teachers in traditional and magnet schools in a large urban school district. *Education and Urban Society,* 33 (1), 60–73.

Gintis, H. (1995). The political economy of school choice. *Teachers College Record,* 96 (3), 492–511.

Godwin, K., Kemerer, F., Martinez, V., & Ruderman, R. (1998). Liberal equity in education: A comparison of choice options. *Social Science Quarterly,* 79 (3), 502–522.

Goldring, E., & Smrekar, C. (2000). Magnet schools and the pursuit of racial balance. *Education and Urban Society,* 33 (1), 17–35.

Harris III, J. J., Ford, D. Y., Wilson, P. I., & Sandidge, R. F. (1991). What should our public choose? The debate over school choice policy. *Education and Urban Society,* 23 (2), 159–174.

Hill, P. T., Pierce, L. C., & Guthrie, J. W. (1997). *Reinventing public education: How contracting can transform America's schools.* Chicago: University of Chicago Press.

Jenkins, J. M., & Dow, J. L. (1996). A primer on charter schools. *International Journal of Educational Reform,* 5 (2), 224–228.

Lightfoot, S. L. (1983). *The good high school: Portraits of character and culture.* New York: Basic Books.

Martin, M. (1991). Trading the known for the unknown: Warning signs in the debate over schools of choice. *Education and Urban Society,* 23 (2), 119–143.

Moe, T. M. (Ed.). (1995). *Private vouchers.* Stanford, CA: Hoover Institution Press.

Nathan, J. (1996). *Charter schools: Creating hope and opportunity for American education.* San Francisco, Jossey-Bass.

Noddings, N. (1984). *Caring: A feminine approach to ethics and moral education.* Berkeley: University of California Press.

Noddings, N. (1992). *The challenge to care in schools: An alternative approach to education.* New York: Teachers College Press.

Noddings, N. (1993). Caring: A feminist perspective. In K. A. Strike & P. L. Ternasky (Eds.), *Ethics for professionals in education: Perspectives for preparation and practice* (pp. 43–53). New York: Teachers College Press.

Noddings, N. (1999). Care, justice, and equity. In M. S. Katz, N. Noddings, & K. A. Strike (eds.), *Justice and caring: The search for common ground in education* (pp. 7–20). New York: Teachers College Press.

Peterkin, R. S., & Jackson, J. E. (1994). Public school choice: Implications for African American students. *Journal of Negro Education,* 63 (1), 126–138.

Pierce v. Society of Sisters, 268 U.S. (1925).

Raywid, M. A. (1998). History and issues of alternative schools. *High School Magazine,* 6, 10–14.

Russo, C. J., & Gordon, W. M. (1996). Home schooling: The in-house alternative. *School Business Affairs,* 62 (12), 16–20.

Schneider, M., Teske, P., & Marschall, M. (2000). *Choosing schools: Consumer choice and the quality of American schools.* Princeton, NJ: Princeton University Press.

Sernak, K. (1998). *School leadership—Balancing power with caring.* New York: Teachers College Press.

Unger, H. G. (1999a). *School choice: How to select the best schools for your children.* New York: Checkmark Books.

Unger, H. G. (1999b). *How to pick a perfect private school.* (Revised Edition). New York: Checkmark Books.

Viteritti, J. P. (1999). *Choosing equality: School choice, the constitution, and civil society.* Washington, DC: Brookings Institution Press.

Webb, J., Wilson, B., Corbett, D., & Mordecai, R. (1993). Understanding caring in context: Negotiating borders and barriers. *The Urban Review,* 25 (1), 25–45.

Conclusion

Sandra Harris, Ph.D.

Someone once said that the purpose of public schools is to provide services to "all the children of all the people"; certainly, a worthy and necessary goal, especially in a democracy, such as the United States. However, there are 53 million school children in America today—53 million children who come from different cultures, different backgrounds; children whose families are very different, who come from different homes and neighborhoods. These children have parents who want different kinds of education for their children. In the 1700s a primary goal of education was for children to be able to read the Bible. Over the years, the goals of education have changed and diversified considerably from Thomas Jefferson's idea in 1779 to "offer free education for three years to nonslave children" (p. 8) and selecting from this group the most talented for further education, to Bill Clinton's Goals 2000, signed in 1994, which had as an overall goal to improve the U.S. economy by educating better workers (Spring, 1996).

Additionally, these 53 million school children represent many different languages as numbers of children who are not proficient in English, but native speakers of another language have grown. In fact, in the 1991–92 school year, at least, 15 different languages were spoken by New York City school students (Spring, 1996). There are children of poverty and children of wealth. Children of politically conservative parents and children of politically liberal parents. Some children come from homes with computer access, books and writing materials available, and, still, today, some of America's children come to school with none of these supports necessary to help them in the schooling process.

Even children who come from very similar homes and backgrounds come to school with very different needs. Some are ready to read, some are not. Some do well in one subject, but poorly in another. Some children are extremely talented in one area, others exhibit their talents in different ways. Fifty three million children cannot all be treated the same. Fifty three million children have many, many different educational needs. The traditional neighborhood public school system cannot be expected to meet all the needs of all the children. Although it can be expected to provide "services to all of America's children," these services, increasingly, are most likely to be successful when offered in a variety of educational settings.

Thus, American parents and American educators are embracing different forms of school choice, emphasizing the need to make informed choices. Parents and educators must understand the elements of caring schools, because it is their child and their professional life that will be nurtured (or not) in that environment. Therefore, in order to make these decisions wisely and ask the right questions, it is imperative that the language of choice be understood.

In looking for "good schools," parents must consider their own child's needs to determine best what is good for their child. While parents and educators certainly need to know the correlates of effective schools, they also need to know what will be most effective for their child, or for their career. School choice is about democracy. It is about giving the greatest educational opportunity available to a child to undergird that child's future success.

Recently, H.R. 1 was passed by the House of Representatives (House passes President Bush's, 2001). Among the provisions of this bill are unprecedented flexibility for parents to remove a child from a low-performing school and send her to a different public school immediately, and supplementary educational services, such as tutoring and summer school programs, have been expanded to include private faith-based providers. While this bill does not provide for tuition vouchers or tax credits that would allow parents to choose to send their children to attend schools in the private sector, it clearly strengthens the foundation that in order to give children a chance, parents must be given a choice to determine which school their child will attend.

The child of the new millennium who is not having educational needs met at the school he or she attends, has more schooling options available than ever before; as do educators when choosing a school in which to teach. While school choice is for everyone interested in education, it is really about children and providing for every child an opportunity to be successful. Whether a parent selects the traditional public neighborhood school, a magnet school, an academic alternative school, charter school, or perhaps a public school contracting with an EMO . . . whether a parent chooses to consider a private independent school, Catholic school, Christian school, or, perhaps, decides to home school . . . by choosing wisely, there is a school for every child in America today.

Chapter References

House passes President Bush's "No Child Left Behind" education bill (H.R.1). (2001, May 23). News Release. Committee on Education and the Workforce. [Online]. Available: *http://www.edworkforce.house.gov/press/press107/hr1ph5301.htm*.

Spring, J. (1996). *American education,* 7th edition. New York: McGraw-Hill.

Contributors

Dr. Betty Alford is an associate professor at Stephen F. Austin State University in Texas, where she directs the Gaining Early Awareness and Readiness for Undergraduate Programs (GEAR UP) project. She is a former public school teacher, counselor, and administrator. Her research interests include school leadership development and factors influencing secondary students' course-taking patterns.

Dr. Carolyn Carr, a former public school counselor and administrator, is an associate professor of educational leadership at Portland State University. Her research has focused on gender and language issues related to school leadership and on principal preparation.

Dr. Lenoar Foster is an associate professor in the Department of Educational Leadership and Counseling at the University of Montana–Missoula. His reserach interests include the principalship and school reform. He has served as a Catholic high school principal and has consulted in secondary education for several Catholic high schools.

Dr. John Gooden is currently an associate professor of Educational Leadership at the University of North Carolina at Charlotte. For 21 years he served as a teacher and administrator in private schools in New York and Massachusetts.

Dr. Sandra Harris has experience in public and private schools as a teacher and administrator. Her research interests include the principalship and schools of choice. She is an assistant professor at Stephen F. Austin State University.

Dr. C. Michelle Hooper is a former public school teacher. She is currently assistant professor of secondary education at Stephen F. Austin State University. Her research interests include racial identity and multicultural education.

Dr. Michael Hopson is a former high school principal. His research interests include educational technology. Dr. Hopson is coordinator of the Principalship program at Stephen F. Austin State University in Texas.

Dr. Raymond A. Horn is an assistant professor of education at Penn State University–Harrisburg. His research interests include post-formal thinking, educational change, educational leadership, and teacher education. His most recent book is *American Standards: Quality Education in a Complex World—The Texas Case.*

Dr. Patrick M. Jenlink is a former public school teacher, guidance counselor, and administrator. He is currently professor of doctoral studies and director of the Educational Research Center at Stephen F. Austin State University. His research interests include caring and social justice in schools, designing educational systems, and educational leadership preparation and practice. Dr. Jenlink has edited books, authored articles, and is currently editor of two journals.

Brian Kasperitis is the director-founder of Kingwood Cove Learning Centre in Houston, Texas. He completed his Master's degree with thesis at Stephen F. Austin State University. Mr. Kasperitis's research interests include homeschooling and adult education.

Dr. Sandra Lowery is a former teacher and superintendent. Her research interests are in the superintendency and educational legal issues. Dr. Lowery is the interim chair of the Department of Secondary Education and Educational Leadership and associate professor at Stephen F. Austin State University.

Dr. Diane Porter Patrick is an assistant professor and director of PK–12 administrator preparation at the University of Texas at Arlington. Dr. Patrick is a former public school teacher and director of PK–12 education at a psychiatric hospital. She is a former member of Texas State Board of Education and Arlington School Board. She has done extensive research on charter schools.

Dr. Garth Petrie is a professor of educational leadership in the doctoral program at Stephen F. Austin State University. He has published numerous articles in journals and chapters in books. His research interests include the principalship.

Dr. Sharon Spall is an associate professor at Western Kentucky University. Previously in public schools, she was a teacher and administrator. Her research interests include homeschooling, qualitative methodologies, and rural education.

Dr. Donnya Stephens is a professor in the Department of Secondary Education and Educational Leadership. She is a former public school teacher and community college professor. Her research interests include mentoring, teacher preparation and practice, and teacher leadership.